THE ART OF SHAPE YOUR CAREER

9 WAYS DRIVING GROWTH & SUCCESS IN THE DIGITAL AGE

SUNIL PILLAI

Chennai • Bangalore

CLEVER FOX PUBLISHING
Chennai, India

Published by CLEVER FOX PUBLISHING 2024
Copyright © Sunil Pillai 2024

All Rights Reserved.
ISBN: 978-93-56488-71-7

This book has been published with all reasonable efforts taken to make the material error-free after the consent of the author. No part of this book shall be used, reproduced in any manner whatsoever without written permission from the author, except in the case of brief quotations embodied in critical articles and reviews.

The Author of this book is solely responsible and liable for its content including but not limited to the views, representations, descriptions, statements, information, opinions and references ["Content"]. The Content of this book shall not constitute or be construed or deemed to reflect the opinion or expression of the Publisher or Editor. Neither the Publisher nor Editor endorse or approve the Content of this book or guarantee the reliability, accuracy or completeness of the Content published herein and do not make any representations or warranties of any kind, express or implied, including but not limited to the implied warranties of merchantability, fitness for a particular purpose. The Publisher and Editor shall not be liable whatsoever for any errors, omissions, whether such errors or omissions result from negligence, accident, or any other cause or claims for loss or damages of any kind, including without limitation, indirect or consequential loss or damage arising out of use, inability to use, or about the reliability, accuracy or sufficiency of the information contained in this book.

Cherishing my mother, the first and best teacher of the universe, helping me survive and grow.

CONTENTS

Foreword .... *vi*
Dedication .... *vii*
Acknowledgments .... *ix*
Introduction .... *xi*
Books In This Series .... *xiii*
Afterword .... *xv*
What Does Shaping Your Career Mean? .... *xvii*

1. **Discovering Self-Awareness** 1
    Chapter 1.1: Understanding Your Transferable Skills 7
    Chapter 1.2: Uncovering Your Interests and Passions 14
    Chapter 1.3: Exploring Childhood Hobbies and Voluntary Work 25
    Chapter 1.4: Identifying Your Ideal Work Environment 30
    Chapter 1.5: Matching Personality Types with Career Paths 34
    Chapter 1.6: Cultivating Curiosity and Problem-Solving Skills 46
2. **Navigating Opportunity Awareness** 51
    Chapter 2.1 Finding What's Best for You 55

Chapter 2.2: Exploring Intriguing Industries and Fields 59
Chapter 2.3: Seeking Advice from Professionals 63
Chapter 2.4: Networking to Connect with Like-Minded Individuals 68
Chapter 2.5: Evaluating Transferable Skills in Different Professions...72

3. **Taking Action Towards Career Success 76**
   Chapter 3.1: Identifying and Overcoming Barriers.........81
   Chapter 3.2: Bridging the Gap With Relevant Education or Experience 86
   Chapter 3.3: Managing Time and Overcoming Procrastination 90
   Chapter 3.4: Embracing Financial Responsibility 95
   Chapter 3.5: Overcoming the Fear of Failure................101
   Chapter 3.6: Building Emotional Resilience 107
4. **Fostering A Career Management 112**
5. **Reflecting On Your Passions: Uncover Your True Career Calling 120**
6. **Embracing Growth Mindset: Cultivating A Learning Attitude 130**
7. **Identifying Your Core Values: Building A Solid Foundation For Career Satisfaction........................... 135**
8. **Setting Meaningful Goals: Creating A Roadmap To Career Success 141**
9. **Seeking Mentorship: Tapping Into The Power Of Guidance And Support.. 147**

FOREWORD

I'll bet that there's one excuse you have in your life that is keeping you away from executing specific actions. They may go from specific reasons like "I'm timid, so I can't get any place in life" to essential reasons like "incredible things don't occur to people like me."

Either way, these reasons are superfluous. Incidentally, it's not the excuses we make that prevent us from getting somewhere. It's simply how our goals are close to nothing and don't test our cutoff points.

Try not to start satisfying your potential tomorrow; do it now, regardless of whether it implies reducing your mid-day break. Truly set these means in motion and start being the individual you wish to be—the individual you're intended to be.

DEDICATION

I had never imagined in my wildest dreams that I would write a book one day. It is more challenging than I thought and more rewarding than I could have ever imagined.

This book is dedicated to the most important people in my life.

My deepest thanks to my late father, K. Madhavan Pillai, a humble being who has always been the greatest inspiration in my life. To my mother, Shanta Pillai, for all the love, care, and motivation whose sacrifice and selfless love cannot be expressed in words, helping me reach where I am today.

My family is my strength, include my brother, Anil Pillai (who is my intellectual supporter and an avid critic), and my sister, Indu, who stands rock solid with me in my endeavours.

My better half, Ajitha, the love of my life, also stood rock solid with me and supported me through thick and thin. My bundle of joy and motivation and the only one who means the world to me, my son, Bhumin. Mr. V R Mohan and Mrs. Usha Mohan for always supporting and encouraging me.

Finally, I extend my gratitude to all those who are family, friends, and mentors (Mr. Sekar Basu, Mr. Sandeep Kapoor and Mr. N Ayappan for kindling my curiosity and guiding me always, leading my way to where I am today) and to all my near ones and colleagues, who wished my success and believed in me, whose names may be missing here but who have been a part and continue to be a part of my journey.

ACKNOWLEDGMENTS

First and foremost, I want to thank God for providing me with the finest parents, inspirational mentors, and a child that anybody could possibly want.

Second, a huge hug to my father, Late Mr. K. Madhavan Pillai, who always blesses me from heaven and is still here to protect me. He was very modest, sweet, loving, and compassionate, and he supported everyone who approached him. My father loved me more than he loved himself, and my mother agreed. I inherited his trait of being a loving and caring parent.

Third, to my mother, Ms. Shanta Pillai, who has been through so much in her life that her tale may inspire people worldwide. Throughout much of her life, my mother worked extremely hard to raise me and my siblings wonderfully and meet all our unreasonable demands, even when circumstances were terrible. Her desire to provide me with an outstanding education and inspire the entire world motivated me to live her dreams. Her never-say-die attitude and will to succeed taught me to be tolerant and resilient.

Her struggle to raise me despite life's setbacks and her encouragement to respect my essence represent who I am now. Thank you so much, Mom!

Acknowledgments

Thank you so much to my son, Master Bhumin S Pillai, for being one of the most crucial buzz moments (when you feel out of this world) in my life. Without him, I would have been content with my mundane life and would not have dared to dream large. He is an electric current flowing through the bulb inside of me. Girik, you were, are, and will always be my one and only love. Thank you so much for being my son.

A heartfelt thank you to my mentors, Sekar Basu, Sandeep Kapoor, and N. Ayyappan, for making my professional path easier and guiding and directing me to where I am now.

Special appreciation to the multi-talented wonder girl Ajitha who appeared out of nowhere and quickly earned a vital place in my life. Most of my interactions with her have been and will continue to be buzz moments for me. Her life path, warrior spirit, many methods, and upbeat attitude inspired me in various ways.

Last but not least, thank **YOU** for picking this book and taking ownership to **shape your career.** After reading this book, I am sure you will understand ***what to achieve***, ***when to achieve*** and ***how to achieve***.

Do not forget to write to me about how this book helped you. Please do leave your feedback on Amazon. It will encourage many people like you to buy this book and inspire them to take responsibility to make their lives happy and content.

Love you all,

Sunil Pillai
sunilkumarpillai@rediffmail.com

INTRODUCTION

Throughout childhood and adulthood, we are grilled to do well to get an appropriate qualification to perform various jobs in the market. We get fascinated with multiple positions, celebrities, and heroes that we see around us and tend to get influenced and dream of becoming one. While we grow up, we want to make decisions. However, we only make a choice that is either available or asked to do.

Even when we get into a job or work in a specific role, we either don't like to continue or are unhappy to continue without knowing the reason. This has been an intriguing question for a long time. I had the opportunity to work in multiple functions and interact with various personalities.

Then, I realised there has been much research done on it, and there are various methods by which we can discover our true selves and get along with our desired careers. There are many aspects to be covered during our initial phase as teenagers. Even as we evolve and venture into unfamiliar professional domains, comprehensive guidance and key steps to align with our true selves and shape our careers are scarce on a single platform, making it challenging to filter essential information.

Introduction

For example, having a mentor to guide us in our short-term and long-term goals and ambitions or when to choose one and having a community to contribute and grade us on our performance. Many scientific methods help us determine our true nature, and we can align with them. We can practice many things to ensure we are portrayed as better and wannabe professionals in this competitive world, which is changing dynamically.

The book is about understanding the essential aspects one can consider to shape or transform one's career. It contains essential guidelines and checks to follow in every phase of his desired career aspiration. There is some information about a few personalities and how they transformed their career by achieving what they are today. The book also includes critical factors for learning and continuous learning.

While flipping through the pages of this book, you will realise that it will educate and guide you about the possibilities you could create after discovering who you are. You could identify factors that made you happy and change your negative belief system (a set of moral codes) that stopped your growth—a structured way of discovering, enhancing and transforming yourself.

BOOKS IN THIS SERIES

1. The Art of Shaping Your Career: Discovering You

Step into the first phase of your personal and professional evolution. *Discovering You* invites readers to embark on an introspective journey to uncover their innate strengths, passions, and potential. Dive deep into self-assessment tools, real-life anecdotes, and exercises designed to illuminate the unique qualities that set you apart. By the end of this guide, you'll clearly understand who you are and the paths best suited for your career journey.

2. The Art of Shaping Your Career: Enhancing You

Building on the foundations set in *Discovering You*, *Enhancing You* is the essential guide to refining and expanding upon your inherent skills and aspirations. This book provides actionable strategies to boost your capabilities, enhance your professional image, and position yourself as an invaluable asset in any industry. Discover the secrets to continuous learning, effective networking, and personal branding, ensuring you remain at the forefront of your career.

3. The Art of Shaping Your Career: Transforming You

The pinnacle of the series *Transforming You* is for those ready to reshape their career trajectory and reinvent themselves in the professional world. Here, readers will be equipped with the techniques and insights to break through personal barriers, overcome stagnation, and pivot towards more fulfilling roles or industries. From fostering a growth mindset to embracing the unknown, this guide offers a blueprint for those daring to transcend their current circumstances and ascend to greater professional heights.

Embark on this transformative journey with *The Art of Shaping Your Career* series, which has been tailored for every stage of your career evolution. Whether discovering your purpose, enhancing your presence, or seeking a total transformation, these guides are your dedicated companions towards a fulfilling professional life.

AFTERWORD

To all the seekers, dreamers, and doers who have accompanied me on this journey, thank you for entrusting me with your time and aspirations.

The inception of *The Art of Shaping Your Career* series was neither a momentary inspiration nor a sudden brainwave. It is a culmination of several years of personal and professional observations. Everywhere I looked, I encountered talented individuals trapped in roles that dimmed their shine or in careers that failed to resonate with their heart's true calling. The recurring question was: "How can one align passion with profession?"

During a quiet evening, reminiscing about my career trajectory—filled with its own set of peaks and valleys—the idea began to take shape. I remembered the countless times I had been lost, the moments when I felt directionless, and the instances where a slight nudge or a piece of advice set me back on the right track. The desire to consolidate those learnings and experiences into a tangible guide became a burning passion.

However, the true inspiration behind this series was a simple belief that every individual is like a unique piece of art. And just like art, they can be shaped, refined, and transformed. We all have the potential for greatness; sometimes, we only need a roadmap to help us navigate our path.

Discovering You was birthed from the idea that understanding oneself is the cornerstone of any meaningful career. *Enhancing You* came from recognising that continuous growth and adaptation are paramount in today's ever-evolving world. Lastly, *Transforming You* is for those audacious souls ready to redefine their boundaries and reshape their destinies.

As you close each book, I sincerely hope you find more than just advice. I hope you find empowerment, inspiration, and, most importantly, a reflection of your true self. May your journey be filled with discovery, enhancement, and transformation. Shape your career, but let it also shape you.

With heartfelt gratitude and best wishes,

Sunil Pillai

WHAT DOES SHAPING YOUR CAREER MEAN?

Synopsis

Shaping your career means actively steering your professional journey towards your goals and aspirations. It involves self-awareness, skill development, strategic planning, and adaptability. Career growth isn't just promotions or raises; it's about personal development and increasing your capacity and impact, through which you can contribute to society and self-development.

For example, imagine you are a software engineer who loves management. Shaping your career might involve seeking leadership roles, gaining relevant qualifications, or leading small projects to demonstrate your capacity to your current organization or the organization you prefer to work in future. Teachers realize they want to impact education policy and work towards a role in educational consulting. To gain a broader business understanding, a project manager takes on roles in operations, sales, etc. An amateur baker turning their passion into a career by opening a bakery. A customer service representative learning programming to move into a tech role. An aspiring executive gaining experience in various business units to understand the company's operation holistically.

Hence, one needs to regularly reassess one's career goals and ensure that his current path aligns with his aspirations. You must stay updated on industry trends, invest in continuous learning and define your career accordingly by regularly investing time in learning new skills or improving existing ones.

Now, the question is understanding the need for change. Change in a career could stem from various factors, such as job dissatisfaction, industry shifts, or personal growth. Embracing change helps you stay relevant and fulfilled. A few things to illustrate are as follows:

- Growing at your company
- Defining your career
- Shifting your skills to stay competitive.
- Thinking career lattice and not ladder
- Thinking strategically about your career
- Discovering your passion
- Understanding your values
- Developing your skills.

Thus, career enhancement must be strategic career thinking, which involves long-term planning, considering market trends, and aligning your career moves with your goals. One must maintain an open mindset and continually update your skills to accommodate changes in your industry. You must recognize your aspirations, identify your strengths, and set career goals. As market demands change, adjusting your skill set is crucial for staying competitive. If we have already started our journey as a professional, then career enhancement involves seeking out lateral opportunities within the organization for a varied skill set and wider perspective.

Why is shaping your career important?

Shaping your career involves carefully planning, developing, and implementing steps towards your desired professional path. It involves making conscious decisions and taking the necessary steps to achieve career objectives rather than leaving things to chance or external forces. The importance of shaping your career stems from its significant impact on personal satisfaction, financial stability, and overall life fulfilment. This concept can be dissected and understood from several perspectives.

1. **Self-fulfillment and Personal Satisfaction**: Career plays a pivotal role in one's sense of self-worth and personal identity. Shaping your career according to your passions, interests, and strengths enables you to engage in work that aligns with your values, leading to higher personal satisfaction and fulfilment.
2. **Financial Stability**: A well-shaped career often leads to better job opportunities and increased earning potential. Financial stability is an important aspect of life as it impacts one's ability to meet needs, save for the future, and achieve certain life goals.
3. **Skill Development**: Shaping your career involves acquiring and honing various skills. Whether technical skills related to a specific job or soft skills like communication, leadership, or problem-solving, these competencies are valuable in workplaces and life.
4. **Adaptability**: In today's fast-changing job market, being proactive about shaping your career equips you with the ability to adapt to changes, learn new skills, and seize emerging opportunities. It fosters resilience and reduces the risk of job insecurity.

5. **Control Over Your Life**: Actively shaping your career gives you control over your life's trajectory. Rather than passively accepting whatever comes your way, you can create your own path and make career decisions that align with your overall life goals.
6. **Contribution to Society**: You will likely excel in your work by shaping your career according to your strengths and passions. This doesn't just benefit you; it also allows you to make meaningful contributions to your workplace and society.
7. **Professional Growth**: Career shaping often involves setting and achieving professional goals, continuous learning, and seeking opportunities for advancement, all of which lead to professional growth.
8. **Long-term Happiness:** Research has shown that people who find meaning and satisfaction in their careers are happier and have better mental health. By shaping your career proactively, you're more likely to find long-term happiness.

In conclusion, shaping your career is crucial to personal and professional development. It's about identifying your interests, skills, and values, setting career goals in alignment with them, and taking action towards these goals. The importance of this process lies in its potential to bring self-fulfilment, financial stability, skill development, adaptability, control over your life, contribution to society, professional growth, and long-term happiness. In essence, shaping your career is integral to shaping your life.

Shaping your career involves three stages in your career:

- Discovering yourself

- Enhancing yourself
- Transforming yourself

Every individual is unique and has unique interests, talents, skills, likings, values and passions, which need to be identified in the first place by various means. Then, we must enhance those interests, passions and skills to elevate ourselves to our next career level. Finally, to transform and transition to the next role. Various steps must be followed, and many things must be considered. You have to adopt new practices and habits, embrace new methods, and leave a few habits and methods which are a roadblock in your growth. This book guides you to follow those key things and guidelines to shape your career.

As shared above, the importance of this process lies in its potential to bring self-fulfilment, financial stability, skill development, adaptability, control over your life, contribution to society, professional growth, and long-term happiness. In essence, shaping your career is integral to shaping your life. Come, let's glide through the discoveries to reach our peak.

Discovering You

Chapter 1

DISCOVERING SELF-AWARENESS

Synopsis

The career development journey is an inward expedition as much as an outward one. Self-awareness is the most fundamental and influential among the internal landscapes you'll navigate. This chapter will guide you in discovering self-awareness and harnessing its transformative influence on your career journey.

Understanding Self-Awareness

Self-awareness is an ongoing journey into understanding your thoughts, emotions, strengths, weaknesses, and motivations. Understanding your wants, desires, flaws, habits, and everything else that makes you tick is at the heart of self-awareness. The more self-aware you are, the easier it will be for you to adjust to changes in your life. This ability to know oneself is the foundation on which you can build many other essential life and career skills, including emotional intelligence, decision-making, self-management, and relationship-building. It's about knowing what makes you unique, what you need to thrive, and how you interact with others.

In a career context, self-awareness helps you make informed decisions that align with your true self, leading to more satisfaction and success. By understanding yourself better, you can align your career with who you are, not just who you think you should be. In this way, you can craft a career that's both successful and deeply fulfilling.

1. **Career Alignment**: Through self-awareness, you identify your strengths, weaknesses, passions, values, and personality type, enabling you to align your career with your true self. This alignment increases the likelihood of satisfaction and success in your chosen career.
2. **Effective Decision-Making**: Self-aware individuals make informed decisions. For instance, understanding your skill gaps may prompt you to pursue further training or education, positioning you for career advancement.
3. **Improved Relationships:** Self-awareness can lead to better professional relationships. Understanding your emotions and reactions can enhance your communication with colleagues, managers, and clients.
4. **Career Advancement**: Self-awareness can lead to better job performance by highlighting areas for improvement and enabling you to leverage your strengths.

Cultivating Self-Awareness

Developing self-awareness is a continuous journey that can be facilitated through various methods.

A step-by-step guide you could follow is as below:

Step 1: Reflection - Spend time reflecting on your thoughts, feelings, and actions. How do you react to challenges? What motivates you? What drains you?

Step 2: Seek Feedback - Gain different perspectives on your strengths and areas of improvement through feedback from mentors, colleagues, friends, and family.

Step 3: Self-Assessment Tools - Tools like personality tests (e.g., Myers-Briggs), strength finder assessments and emotional intelligence tests can provide valuable insights.

Step 4: Mindfulness Practice - Increase your awareness of your inner world by engaging in meditation, yoga, or writing.

Step 5: Constant Learning and Adaptation - Self-awareness is an ongoing journey. Continually learn, adapt, and grow.

For example: Consider Maria, a hardworking manager who often feels stressed and unsatisfied. Through self-awareness, she realizes that while she's excellent at executing tasks, she finds more fulfilment in creative problem-solving and strategic planning. This revelation could guide her toward roles that align better with her natural inclinations and passions.

A few other real-life examples are :

1. Oprah Winfrey: Oprah Winfrey, the media mogul, is a powerful example of self-awareness. Born in an underprivileged family, Oprah's early life was filled with hardships, but she did not let that define her future. She recognized her unique strength in connecting with people. This quality turned her into a globally recognized talk show host. Her self-awareness allowed her to see beyond the standard career path.
She started a talk show that delved into societal and personal issues. This unique approach resonated with millions of viewers and transformed the landscape of television talk shows. Her ongoing journey of self-awareness and personal growth continues to inform her career decisions, leading to the launch of her OWN Network and her role as a thought leader in personal development.
2. Elon Musk: Elon Musk, the founder of Tesla, SpaceX, and several other innovative companies, demonstrates a high degree of self-awareness in his professional life. He is known for his ability to evaluate his assumptions critically and to understand his strengths and weaknesses. Despite criticism and immense obstacles, he persisted in industries like electric cars and private space exploration because he understood that his strength lay in his ability to innovate and challenge traditional boundaries.
In interviews, Musk admitted that he needed to work on his communication and emotions—a vital recognition of a self-aware leader. His understanding of his capabilities and areas for improvement has allowed him to become one of the most successful entrepreneurs of the 21st century.

3. Indra Nooyi: Indra Nooyi, the former CEO of PepsiCo, exhibits strong self-awareness in her leadership style. Nooyi recognized early in her career that her passion and strength lay in strategic thinking. She moved from product management roles to strategy roles, ultimately leading her to the CEO position.
Nooyi is also noted for her ability to balance multiple identities as a corporate leader, mother, immigrant, and woman. She has spoken about the challenges of these roles, reflecting a keen sense of self-awareness. This self-awareness has allowed her to navigate the complexities of leading a global company while staying true to herself.
4. Steve Jobs: The late co-founder of Apple, Steve Jobs, had a unique perspective on life and business that set him apart from many other entrepreneurs. Jobs was famously introspective, often discussing the importance of looking inward for answers. His self-awareness was particularly evident in his product development approach.
Jobs once said, "People don't know what they want until you show it to them." This was not a mere disregard for market research; it was a deep understanding of his strengths in envisioning future trends. His self-awareness about his abilities in design and innovation led to the creation of ground breaking products like the iPhone, iPad, and iPod, which revolutionised their respective markets.

Accepting your imperfections and being open to feedback is critical to developing self-awareness. Rely on both self-reflection and external input for a comprehensive understanding of yourself. But it is imperative one should maintain the balance between introspection and feedback. Self-awareness is a lifelong journey, and patience is of utmost priority. Be patient with your progress.

- Regularly practice reflection.
- Seek feedback from various sources.
- Use self-assessment tools.
- Engage in mindfulness practices.
- Commit to continual learning and adaptation.

The journey of self-awareness is a powerful expedition that can guide you to a fulfilling career. It illuminates the path to career choices more aligned with your genuine interests, values, and abilities. It enables you to work on your weaknesses and leverage your strengths. It aids you in building healthier workplace relationships and navigating your career trajectory more effectively. Self-aware individuals are better able to steer their careers in satisfying and rewarding directions, perform at a higher level, and build stronger relationships, leading to increased career success.

CHAPTER 1.1: UNDERSTANDING YOUR TRANSFERABLE SKILLS

1. Understanding Transferable Skills

Transferable skills, or your acquired talents, commonly called "portable skills," may be used in various occupations and sectors. You've also developed abilities that can be used in multiple jobs and industries. They can be soft skills like leadership, communication, and problem-solving or hard skills like proficiency in a foreign language or competency in data analysis.

Self-awareness isn't only about recognizing your passions, values, and aspirations. It also involves understanding your skills that can be applied across different jobs or career fields. These are your transferable skills. This sub-chapter will guide you in identifying and leveraging these skills.

In the context of career development, transferable skills are abilities and talents that are relevant and beneficial across different jobs and industries. They are often acquired and honed through various life and work experiences. Transferable skills are essential for career success as they showcase your versatility and adaptability to potential employers.

There are many types of transferable skills, each with unique relevance and importance. However, they can be broadly categorized into three types: people skills, technical skills, and conceptual skills.

People Skills: People skills, sometimes known as "soft skills," include a variety of aptitudes that promote interpersonal interaction and communication. They are the interpersonal attributes that you use to interact with others effectively. These are the skills related to interacting effectively with others. Communication, teamwork, empathy, conflict resolution, leadership, and customer service are crucial people skills. These are highly sought after in virtually every industry because, in most jobs, you will have to interact with people in one way or another.

Key people skills include **empathy, active listening, communication, conflict resolution, teamwork, leadership, and customer service.**

Technical Skills: These are the practical abilities and knowledge needed to perform specific tasks, often related to information technology, machinery, language, or tools. Technical skills are usually acquired through education, training, or on-the-job experience. They are often specific to a particular role or industry. For instance, software programming, machinery operation, or expertise in foreign languages are all examples of technical skills. A programmer's technical skills include knowledge of Python or Java, while a graphic designer might be proficient in using Adobe Illustrator or Photoshop. Although they seem relevant to only specific sectors, you'd be surprised how often these skills can be applied in different fields. Technical skills are proof of your ability to perform tasks essential to a particular role, making you a valuable asset to employers.

Conceptual Skills: These include your ability to work with ideas and concepts. Problem-solving, strategic thinking, creativity, and analytical skills fall under this category. Employers respect employees who can think critically and solve problems regardless of the job. A manager with excellent conceptual skills can see how all the parts of a company work together, enabling them to make decisions that benefit the company. These skills are highly valued in leadership roles but are helpful at any career stage. They demonstrate your ability to think critically, solve problems, and contribute to a company's strategic direction.

Understanding your transferable skills is crucial in shaping your career for several reasons. First, they enhance your employability. When you can demonstrate to potential employers that you possess skills that can benefit their organization, you increase your chances of getting hired.

Second, they aid in career transitions. Your transferable skills can be your most significant selling point if you're considering changing industries. For instance, your communication and leadership skills are transferable and highly relevant if you're moving from a teaching position to a corporate training role.

Third, recognizing your transferable skills can boost your confidence and help you understand your worth in the job market. It gives you a solid foundation to negotiate salaries, promotions, and job roles.

To effectively leverage your transferable skills, you must first identify them. Reflect on your past experiences, roles, and responsibilities. Consider various life situations, including volunteer work, hobbies, or even challenging personal events.

Once you've identified your skills, articulate them clearly in your CV, cover letters, and interviews. Use specific examples to demonstrate how you've used these skills in the past.

In conclusion, understanding your transferable skills is crucial to career development. By identifying and leveraging these skills, you can differentiate yourself in the competitive job market, successfully navigate career transitions, and steer your career towards your desired path.

2. Identifying Your Transferable Skills: A Step-by-Step Guide You May Follow

Step 1: Inventory Your Skills - List all the skills you've gained from your work experience, education, hobbies, and volunteer activities. Don't limit yourself to technical skills; include soft skills and personal attributes.

Step 2: Classify Your Skills - Group your skills into categories like 'communication,' 'leadership,' 'technical expertise,' 'project management,' and so on.

Step 3: Validate Your Skills - Seek feedback from colleagues, mentors, or teachers about your skillset. Their perspectives can add validity to your self-assessment.

Step 4: Prioritize - Identify which skills are most relevant to your career goals.

3. Leveraging Transferable Skills: An Example

Transferable skills, as the name suggests, are abilities that can be transferred and applied to various job roles across different industries. They are the expertise, know-how, and aptitudes you have acquired through multiple experiences not tied to one specific function or industry. Leveraging these skills is about recognizing their value and utilizing them effectively to shape and navigate your career path.

Leveraging Transferable Skills

Leveraging your transferable skills involves several key steps:

Identification: Reflect on your experiences in previous roles, volunteering, education, hobbies, or sports. What are the skills that helped you excel? These can range from teamwork and leadership to time management, analytical thinking, and customer service.

Articulation: Once you've identified your transferable skills, learn to articulate them effectively. This means explaining what the skill is, how you've used it in the past, and how it can benefit a new role or industry. You need to be able to tell your story in a way that makes these skills tangible and relevant to potential employers.

Presentation: Your résumé, cover letter, and LinkedIn profile are all professional mediums where you should highlight these talents. Highlight instances where you have demonstrated these skills in your previous roles.

Development: Never stop building your skill set. Keep looking for opportunities to improve and add to your transferable skills through professional development, continued education, and new experiences.

The Role of Transferable Skills in Shaping Your Career

Leveraging transferable skills plays a crucial role in shaping your career. They provide the foundation for pivoting to new positions or industries. For instance, if you're looking to make a career switch, your transferable skills can help bridge the gap between where you are and where you want to be. In uncertain times or during economic downturns, transferable skills can be the key to staying employable and relevant. They're the skills that can transfer across industries and help you land a job, even when your specific industry is struggling.

In career progression, transferable skills are the ones that usually pave the way for advancement. These skills help you become a better leader, communicate effectively with clients, and successfully manage projects. They make you a valuable asset to any organization.

Let's look at John, a former teacher transitioning to corporate training. He has strong skills in presentation, curriculum development, and understanding individual learning styles—all transferable skills. John can leverage these in his new career, allowing him to excel despite changing fields.

In conclusion, understanding and leveraging your transferable skills is not just beneficial; it's a necessity in the modern job market. They are the bedrock upon which you can build a successful and flexible career. By identifying and harnessing these skills, you are enhancing your employability and shaping a robust career trajectory that can withstand and adapt to the changing employment landscape.

5. Tips and Advice

- Continuous Learning: As you progress in your career, continue to add and refine your transferable skills.
- Be Adaptable: Be open to the idea that your skills can be applied in many contexts.
- Identify your most potent transferable skills.
- Recognize the transferable skills you need to improve.
- Consider ways to use your transferable skills to seize career opportunities.

Determine any external factors that could inhibit the use of your transferable skills.

Promote Your Skills: Include your transferable skills or adaptable abilities in your resume, cover letter, and interviews.

CHAPTER 1.2: UNCOVERING YOUR INTERESTS AND PASSIONS

Synopsis

Uncovering your interests and passions is essential for personal fulfilment and pivotal for career development. This discovery forms the core of self-awareness, the foundation for building a satisfying career that aligns with your authentic self. Many people go through their entire working lives without discovering what truly inspires them, ending up in careers that provide monetary benefits but lack personal fulfilment. This chapter seeks to change that narrative.

As defined by psychologists, self-awareness involves understanding one's emotions, strengths, weaknesses, needs, and impulses. It's a realization of what you love and where your passions lie. In career development, self-awareness encompasses your understanding of your interests and how these relate to your career choices and satisfaction. Without this key element, you may find yourself like a ship without a rudder, directionless and prone to the changing winds of circumstance.

Interests and passions are unique to every individual, forming a significant part of one's identity. Interests are subjects or activities that draw your curiosity. Passions are deeper, more intense interests that generate excitement and drive you to achieve more. For instance, you might be interested in technology. However, your passion could be specifically directed towards cybersecurity, leading you towards a career as a cybersecurity analyst.

It's essential to understand that this process doesn't happen overnight. Uncovering your interests and passions is a journey of self-discovery that takes time and patience. You must dig deep into your past, observe your present, and visualize your future. You might stumble upon some passions easily, while others may take more time and exploration to identify.

In this journey, remember to be patient with yourself. Not all interests transform into passions, and not all passions can be turned into a career. You must consider your skills, the job market, and many other factors. But do not be disheartened. This chapter will guide you through aligning your interests and passions with viable career paths.

Whether at the beginning of your career, thinking about a career change, or seeking more profound satisfaction in your current role, understanding your interests and passions is a step towards creating a fulfilling professional life. By identifying what inspires and motivates you, you can make career choices that align and correspond with your authentic self, leading to greater satisfaction and success.

As you journey through this chapter, keep an open mind, be honest with yourself, and remember that the objective is not merely to make a living but to create a life that reflects your passions and interests. You're not just searching for a job or a career. You're crafting a career that integrates your skills, interests, and passions—a career that truly matters and is close to you and your dreams. This isn't just about making money; it's about making your life count, which always will resonate with you.

Definition of Interests and Passions: Interests and passions, though often used interchangeably, are distinct concepts that play pivotal roles in our lives and careers. They drive our decisions, shape our experiences, and ultimately lead us down different paths. This section will comprehensively understand these two terms, illuminating their differences and importance in career development.

Interests: Interests are topics or activities that naturally pique our curiosity and attention. They could range from artistic pursuits like painting or writing, intellectual pursuits like philosophy or psychology, practical pursuits like cooking or carpentry, or recreational activities like hiking or birdwatching. Our interests often form the backbone of our hobbies, the activities we engage in during our free time.

But interests are not just idle pastimes. They can provide insights into potential career paths. For example, an interest in writing could lead to a career as a journalist, author, or copywriter. In contrast, an interest in hiking could open doors to outdoor guiding or environmental conservation work. When we align our work with our interests, we find greater satisfaction and engagement in our professional lives.

Passions: Passions take interests a step further. They are deep-seated interests that are accompanied by an intense emotional connection. You feel compelled to pursue a passion—something that fills you with energy and excitement. Passions are often so integral to our identity that they can feel like part of our very being.

When passion is at play, people often describe losing track of time and becoming completely engrossed in the activity they are engaged in. This state is often referred to as being "in the flow." For example, a person passionate about painting could spend hours working on a piece, forgetting about meals and not noticing the passing time. This same person might consider a career as a professional artist, not just because they like painting, but because they can't imagine a fulfilling life without it.

Understanding the difference between interests and passions is crucial in making career choices. While an interest might make a job bearable, a passion can make it feel fulfilling and worthwhile. For instance, you might be interested in numbers and hence become an accountant. However, if you're passionate about animals, your career might not fulfil you in the long run. Perhaps a career in veterinary science, wildlife conservation, or a similar field would bring you greater satisfaction.

Passions have the power to motivate us to drive us to go the extra mile. A job that aligns with our passions will not feel like work but an extension of our very selves. This is why uncovering our true passions is important when thinking about our careers.

However, it's crucial to note that passions often require cultivation. They start as interests that can evolve into passions through exploration, learning, and dedication. It's also important to understand that not all passions suit a career path. Some passions might serve better as recreational activities or hobbies that provide relief and balance in our lives.

In conclusion, interests and passions are significant driving forces in our lives. Interests are subjects or activities we enjoy, while passions are those deep-seated interests that ignite enthusiasm and drive us. By understanding these principles, we can make informed career decisions, leading to more satisfying and fulfilling professional lives. As we continue this journey of self-awareness, we'll explore how to uncover our interests and passions and incorporate them into our career paths.

The Role of Interests and Passions in Career Choices: Interests and passions are pivotal in shaping our career paths. They steer us toward professions where we can find joy, satisfaction, and fulfilment. Our interests draw us towards certain areas and subjects, while our passions intensify these attractions, transforming them into driving forces that propel our career journeys. Using illustrative examples, let's delve deeper into how these elements influence career decisions.

A critical first step in any career path is figuring out what you love to do—pinpointing your interests. For instance, a person who has always been fascinated by space and the celestial bodies might be interested in astronomy. This interest could lead them to study astronomy or astrophysics, eventually opening doors to a career as an astronomer or a space researcher.

Interests can also lead us to identify problems that we want to solve. Suppose someone has an interest in climate change and sustainable living. In that case, this interest can influence their career path, leading them to become environmental scientists, sustainability consultants, or renewable energy engineers.

Passions, on the other hand, are the elements that can set your career ablaze. They add an emotional component to your interests, converting them into powerful motivations. Let's consider an individual with a passion for storytelling and a deep love for literature. This passion might lead them to a career as a novelist, a screenplay writer, or a journalist.

Passions can also push you to create unique career paths. For example, someone passionate about health and cooking might not be satisfied with a typical career in either field. Instead, they might combine their passions to become a nutritionist who runs a healthy cooking blog or even a private chef specializing in dietary-specific meals.

The interplay of interests and passions can be seen in individuals who turn their hobbies into careers. Take the example of a person who loves photography. They start by taking pictures for pleasure during their free time, an interest that gradually evolves into a passion. Over time, they might decide to take the plunge and convert this passion into a career, becoming a professional photographer.

However, it's crucial to recognize that the link between interests, passions, and careers isn't always linear. Not every interest or passion can or should be turned into a career. For instance, someone might have a passion for playing the piano but not want to pursue a career as a professional musician. Instead, they might find satisfaction in a music-related career, such as a music teacher or a music therapist, or they might choose a completely different career path, retaining piano playing as a cherished hobby.

Moreover, sometimes passions emerge from career experiences. A person might enter a career due to a general interest and develop a passion for a particular aspect of their job over time. For instance, a software engineer might discover a passion for data analysis after working on a few data-related projects.

In conclusion, interests and passions significantly influence career paths. They guide us towards professions that resonate with our personalities and help us find genuine satisfaction in our work. We can create a fulfilling professional life that mirrors our inner selves by aligning our careers with our interests and passions.

Identifying Your Interests: Identifying your interests is a key step towards carving out a fulfilling career path. It can provide valuable insights into the kind of work you find stimulating and enjoyable. Here is a step-by-step guide to help you identify your interests, illuminated with examples for better understanding:

Step 1: Self-reflection - The journey of identifying interests begins with self-reflection. Spend time thinking about the activities, subjects, and ideas that excite and engage you. Do you love reading about ancient civilizations, trying new recipes, or perhaps designing web pages? This first step is about broad exploration, so feel free to jot down as many activities as come to mind.

For example, if you find yourself eagerly awaiting your home decor magazine, spending your free time rearranging furniture or browsing design websites, you might have an interest in interior design.

Step 2: Look for patterns - Once you have a list, analyze it for patterns. Do your interests lean towards creative activities like painting or writing? Or are you more drawn to analytical tasks, such as solving puzzles or programming? Understanding these patterns can help you discern the broader themes in your interests.

Consider a person who enjoys hiking, gardening, and reading books on environmental science. A common pattern here is a love for nature and the outdoors.

Step 3: Consider your skills - Interests often align with our skills, but not always. You might be interested in something because you're good at it, or you might be motivated to develop new skills because of your interest in a particular area.

For instance, someone interested in animated movies might learn animation software to create short films. The key here is to understand whether your interests are also areas where you have existing skills or would like to develop them.

Step 4: Feedback from others - Sometimes, others can provide valuable insights into our interests. Friends, family, or colleagues might have observed you getting excited about certain topics or activities. Their observations can complement your self-assessment and offer a more holistic view.

For example, your friends might have noticed your knack for picking up languages and your enjoyment in doing so, even if you haven't recognized it as an interest yourself.

Step 5: Validation through experiences - The best way to confirm an interest is to engage in it. Volunteer work, internships, classes, or workshops can provide hands-on experience in your area of interest. These experiences can either deepen your interest or help you realize that something you thought you were interested in isn't as appealing as you imagined.

A person interested in event planning might decide to join the organizing committee of a local festival. The experience would give them a realistic understanding of what event planning involves and whether it truly interests them.

Step 6: Regular review and update: Interests can evolve over time, and it›s essential to revisit and update your list regularly. Changes in life circumstances, exposure to new experiences, or gaining new knowledge can all lead to the development of new interests or the fading of old ones.

Identifying your interests isn't a one-time task but an ongoing process of self-discovery. Whether you're at the beginning of your career journey or at a point of transition, understanding your interests can guide your path, offering signposts towards fulfilling opportunities and, ultimately, towards a career that aligns with who you are

Turning Interests into Passions: Interests are often the seeds of passions. Interests can be likened to the spark that lights the fire and passions to the roaring flame that ensues. A passion is not merely an interest you enjoy. It deeply resonates with you, a pursuit that can provide profound personal satisfaction and significantly shape your career. Let's delve into how interests can evolve into passions and their transformative role in our lives and careers.

An interest can evolve into a passion through immersion, practice, and exploration. When you consistently engage with an area of interest, you delve deeper into its nuances, complexities, and challenges. This continual engagement and the joy or sense of fulfilment it brings can gradually transform an interest into a passion.

Consider the example of a person who enjoys sketching. Over time, as they immerse themselves in sketching more often, studying art, exploring different techniques, and challenging themselves with complex projects, this interest could blossom into a passion for art. The sketcher might then pursue a career as a graphic artist, illustrator, or art teacher, using their passion as a guiding force in their professional life.

When identified and nurtured, passions play a crucial role in personal satisfaction and career fulfilment. A passion can make you feel alive, motivated, and connected to a purpose larger than yourself. In the realm of career development, passions act as magnetic north, guiding you toward roles and industries where you will not only excel but also find profound satisfaction and meaning.

Take the example of someone with a deep passion for environmental conservation. Their passion could lead them to pursue careers in environmental policy, research, education, or advocacy. Their work would not only provide them with a paycheck but also a sense of purpose and a deep personal satisfaction from knowing they are contributing to a cause they care deeply about.

Passions also fuel resilience and persistence, qualities that are particularly valuable in our professional lives. When you're passionate about your work, you're more likely to overcome challenges, persist in the face of setbacks, and strive for excellence.

For example, an entrepreneur passionate about bringing a unique product to market will likely remain resilient, adaptable, and committed despite the myriad challenges of launching a startup.

However, it's crucial to recognize that passions require nurturing. They need time, space, and the right resources to flourish. This might mean seeking education or training, finding mentors, joining relevant organizations, or simply allocating regular time to engage with your passion.

Furthermore, remember that not all passions need to translate into a career. For some, pursuing a passion outside of work can provide a fulfilling balance to their professional life. A software engineer might find balance and satisfaction in their passion for photography without turning it into their profession.

Ultimately, interests and passions are deeply interwoven with our identity. They are a vital part of who we are and how we engage with the world. By nurturing our interests and allowing them to evolve into passions, we can create a life and career filled with purpose, satisfaction, and joy.

CHAPTER 1.3: EXPLORING CHILDHOOD HOBBIES AND VOLUNTARY WORK

Synopsis

Exploring our childhood hobbies and participation in voluntary work can provide valuable insights into our interests, passions, and potential career paths. These activities can reveal natural inclinations, skills, and values that we may not be conscious of yet can significantly influence our career satisfaction and success.

Childhood Hobbies: Childhood hobbies are activities we engage in purely for the joy they bring us, free from external pressures or expectations. These hobbies can offer clues to inherent interests and talents. They may highlight areas where we naturally excel and derive satisfaction, which is crucial for career fulfilment.

For example, in my childhood, I loved assembling and dismantling toys. Thus, it helped me grow up to become an engineer, applying this natural interest in understanding how things work. Also, it helps to develop innovative solutions. Similarly, a child who enjoys storytelling might become a successful author, screenwriter, or video game designer, using their innate creativity to weave compelling narratives.

Childhood hobbies can also reflect our fundamental values and preferred working styles. For instance, team sports might suggest an appreciation for collaboration and competitiveness, attributes valuable in many professional settings. Solitary activities like reading or drawing might hint at a preference for independent work and deep focus, which can guide a person towards specific careers and away from others.

However, it's essential to consider these hobbies in the context of our adult selves. Interests can change over time, and what excites us as children may not excite us as adults. Childhood hobbies serve as a starting point for self-exploration, not a definitive roadmap for our career.

Voluntary Work: Voluntary work refers to the unpaid activities or services one provides, often aimed at benefiting a community, cause, or organization. Voluntary work can reveal our passions, strengths, and values, making it an invaluable tool for self-discovery and career development.

Engaging in voluntary work can uncover passions we might not have been aware of. For example, someone volunteering at an animal shelter might discover a deep-seated passion for animal welfare, guiding them towards a career in veterinary medicine, animal law, or non-profit management.

Voluntary work also allows us to develop and showcase transferrable skills. For example, organizing a fundraising event can demonstrate project management, communication, and leadership skills. These skills can be highlighted on resumes and job interviews, making voluntary work a practical strategy for career advancement.

Volunteering exposes us to different environments, roles, and causes, expanding our understanding of potential career paths. A volunteer role in a hospital might inspire someone to pursue a career in healthcare, while volunteering for a political campaign might lead to a career in public policy.

Lastly, volunteering reflects our values, as we tend to volunteer for causes we care about. These values, such as environmental conservation, social justice, or community development, can guide us towards careers where we can live and express these values.

Childhood hobbies and voluntary work can act as mirrors, reflecting our interests, passions, skills, and values. By exploring these areas, we gain a deeper understanding of ourselves, empowering us to make informed, authentic, and satisfying career choices.

Step 1: Unearthing Your Childhood Hobbies -

Let's start by journeying back to your childhood days. What activities did you gravitate towards in your free time? Write them down in a notebook or a digital document.

List all your childhood hobbies: Spend some time to remember and note down all your childhood hobbies. List them all, whether it was reading, painting, playing a musical instrument, or even organizing your toy collection.

Reflect on each hobby: Next, ponder on each hobby, one at a time. What did you enjoy about it? Did it involve problem-solving? Creativity? Working with others? Here's where you start identifying the underlying skills and preferences related to your hobbies.

Connect the dots: Now, align these interests and skills with potential career paths. A love for storytelling might align with careers in writing, marketing, or film-making, while a penchant for problem-solving can lend itself well to careers in engineering or programming.

Remember the case of Steve Jobs, the co-founder of Apple. Jobs' childhood interest in calligraphy didn't directly dictate his career. However, it later influenced the typography and aesthetics of Apple's user interfaces, setting them apart in the technology market.

Step 2: Delving Into Voluntary Work -

Voluntary work can provide key insights into your career path. The fact that these activities are performed voluntarily, without any monetary incentives, often implies that they're driven by intrinsic motivations, values, or passions.

List all your voluntary experiences: Whether it was volunteering at a local library, a nursing home, an animal shelter, or organizing a fundraising event, jot down all your volunteering experiences.

Reflect on each experience: What did you learn from each experience? What skills did you acquire or use? What did you enjoy about it? What values did these activities reflect?

Apply your insights: Now, explore how these experiences could translate into a career. You might thrive in event planning or non-profit management if you enjoy organising charity events.

If tutoring underprivileged children resonated with you, consider education or social work as potential career paths.

For instance, Bill Gates, co-founder of Microsoft, had a long history of community involvement and charity work. He translated this passion for giving into his career, culminating in forming the Bill and Melinda Gates Foundation, one of the world's largest and most impactful charitable organizations.

CHAPTER 1.4: IDENTIFYING YOUR IDEAL WORK ENVIRONMENT

Synopsis

In the pursuit of career success and satisfaction, the importance of identifying your ideal work environment cannot be overstated. This facet of self-awareness helps ensure that you find not only a job you're skilled at but also a setting where you can thrive and feel fulfilled.

The Essence of a Work Environment: A work environment refers to a workplace's physical and social characteristics. It encompasses factors like the organizational culture, work hours, pace of work, degree of collaboration or autonomy, physical layout, degree of formalism, and even aspects like organizational stability and opportunities for growth.

Why is this important? Because even the most enticing job can turn out to be unsatisfactory if the work environment is incompatible with your personality, work style, or life circumstances. Hence, identifying your ideal work environment is as crucial as determining the type of work you want to do.

The Role of Work Environment in Career Choices:

Consider the story of John, a highly skilled software engineer who loves solving complex coding problems. He takes up a job in a bustling tech start-up, drawn by the exciting projects. However, the start-up's fast-paced, competitive environment, long hours, and constant urgency leave John feeling drained and dissatisfied. Perhaps John would thrive better in a stable corporate setting or a remote work arrangement where he can solve his coding puzzles in a more relaxed, autonomous manner.

This example illustrates how the work environment can significantly impact job satisfaction and career success. Therefore, it's essential to contemplate what kind of work environment you'd thrive in before making career decisions.

Identifying Your Ideal Work Environment:

Self-reflection: Start by thinking about your past experiences. What settings have you felt most productive, comfortable, or satisfied? Consider various aspects: physical setting (busy office vs quiet workspace), work style (team-based vs. independent work), work hours (flexible vs. fixed), organizational culture (competitive vs. cooperative), and pace of work (fast-paced vs. steady).

Assess your personality and preferences: Use personality tests, like the Myers-Briggs Type Indicator (MBTI) or the Big Five Personality traits, to gain insights into your personality. Are you introverted or extroverted? Do you prefer routine or variety? Are you competitive or cooperative? These insights can guide you towards suitable work environments.

Lifestyle and personal circumstances: Your ideal work environment should also align with your personal life and goals.

Do you have family commitments that require flexible hours or remote work? Are you seeking a job that allows for extensive travel? Do you thrive in job security, or are you more attracted to the risk and reward of start-ups?

Skills and career goals: Finally, consider your skills, career goals, and the type of work you'll be doing. Specific environments may be more conducive to certain kinds of work. If you're a graphic designer, a creative, collaborative, and visually stimulating environment might be ideal.

By taking the time to identify your ideal work environment, you position yourself to find not just a job but a place where you can truly shine. Remember, our environment significantly impacts our mental health, motivation, and performance. So, choose a setting that feels right for you. After all, we spend a third of our lives at work; it's worth investing the time to make it as satisfying and enjoyable as possible.

> **Guidelines to Identify Your Ideal Work Environment**
>
> Here are some steps to help you identify your ideal work environment:
>
> **Evaluate past experiences**: Reflect on your past roles and identify what you liked or disliked about the work environment. This can give you insights into what type of environment suits you best.
>
> **Define your needs**: Are you someone who thrives in a dynamic, fast-paced environment, or do you prefer a stable, predictable routine? Do you prefer to work independently or in a team?

Answering these questions might help you identify what you need in a work environment.

Consider your values: Your work environment should align with your values. For example, if work-life balance is essential to you, you may not thrive in a work environment that requires overtime frequently.

Analyze your work style: Understanding your work style can help you identify the kind of environment you'd flourish in. For example, you might thrive in an open and collaborative environment if you're creative.

Knowing your ideal work environment is crucial in shaping your career. It helps you choose a career that aligns with your personality, interests, and values, leading to job satisfaction and success.

CHAPTER 1.5: MATCHING PERSONALITY TYPES WITH CAREER PATHS

Synopsis

Every person has a unique blend of attributes, traits, and characteristics that make up their personality. These elements can influence our likes, dislikes, interactions with others, and, significantly, our career choices. In this chapter, we delve into the science of matching personality types with career paths, explore their importance, and shed light on their nuanced differences. A comprehensive understanding of your personality type can give you a wealth of insight into your ideal career path.

Example: An introverted individual might excel in a career that requires detailed, solitary work, such as a researcher or a writer. Conversely, extroverted individuals might thrive in a bustling, people-oriented environment like sales or event management.

Definition of Personality Types and Career Paths

In general, the psychological classification of different types of individuals based on their distinct patterns of thinking, feeling, and behaving is called Personality type. Some well-known personality type theories include Carl Jung's analytical psychology theory, Katharine Cook Briggs and her daughter Isabel Briggs

Myers' Myers-Briggs Type Indicator (MBTI), and the Big Five personality traits theory, among others.

Career paths, on the other hand, are professional journeys that individuals navigate throughout their working lives. They encompass various roles, jobs, and positions a person might undertake within one or multiple fields, industries, or sectors.

Matching Personality Types with Career Paths

Matching personality types with career paths involves aligning an individual's inherent traits, tendencies, and preferences with a profession's requirements, expectations, and work environment. This alignment can be as broad as choosing between a career that requires interaction and communication with others (for extroverted individuals) versus one that requires solitude and concentration (for introverted individuals). It can also be as nuanced as identifying specific roles within a career path that best match your personality traits. For instance, in the field of software development, a highly organized and detail-oriented person might thrive as a quality assurance analyst. In contrast, a highly imaginative and solution-oriented person may excel as a software developer.

Importance of Matching Personality Types with Career Paths

Recognizing your personality type aids in aligning your career path with your innate tendencies, leading to higher job satisfaction, improved performance, and better overall mental health. Here's how:

Job Satisfaction: When you work in a role that aligns with your personality type, you're likely to enjoy what you do, leading to higher job satisfaction.

Performance: You're more likely to excel in a job that matches your personality because it often means you're using your natural strengths and abilities.

Retention: If you're in a job that suits your personality, you're likely to remain in that job for a longer period. This leads to career stability and progression.

Work-life Balance: A mismatch between your job demands and your personality can create stress and affect your work-life balance.

In conclusion, understanding your personality type is a vital part of your career development process. It can help guide your career choices, from broad industry selection to specific job roles. Matching your personality type with your career path is not about restricting your options; instead, it's about knowing yourself better, understanding where you can thrive, and creating a fulfilling and successful career.

Tip: Be open and honest when answering these assessments to ensure the most accurate results.

Aligning Your Personality Type with Your Career Path

Once you understand your personality type, you can explore which careers might be a good match. Websites such as O*Net Online offer tools to match your personality type with potential careers. Remember, while your personality type can provide direction, it does not dictate your options.

Example: An individual identified as an INFJ (Introverted, Intuitive, Feeling, Judging) might thrive in careers that require compassion, idealism, and a focus on long-term goals, such as social work, counselling, or non-profit work.

- Strengths: Detail-oriented, excellent problem-solving skills
- Weaknesses: Discomfort with public speaking, struggles with multitasking
- Opportunities: Growing need for data analysts, the chance to work remotely
- Threats: High competition, need for continual learning due to rapid industry changes

Constant Reflection and Adjustment

Understanding your personality type and aligning it with your career path is not a one-time event but a continual process of self-discovery and adjustment. As you grow and change, your career needs and wants might shift as well. Maintain flexibility and openness to change.

One may follow the few quick guidelines below:

- Understand your personality type: Utilize assessments like the MBTI or the Big Five
- Research various job possibilities that correspond to your personality type
- Apply a SWOT analysis to your top career choices.
- Be open to change and continuous learning

- Revisit and reassess regularly
- Understand Your Personality Type:
  - Take reputable personality assessments.
  - Reflect on your preferences, strengths, and weaknesses.
- Research Career Options:
  - Explore careers that align with your personality type.
  - Consider how different work environments and roles might fit with your characteristics.
- Consider Multiple Factors:
  - Balance personality insights with other important factors like skills, interests, values, and market demand.
- Seek Professional Guidance:
  - Consider consulting a career counsellor who can help interpret assessment results and guide career planning.
- Stay Flexible:
  - Remember that personality is not deterministic; it's one piece of the puzzle.
  - Be open to exploring various paths and continue to reassess as you grow and change.
- Avoid Stereotyping:
  - Don't pigeonhole yourself or others strictly based on personality type.
  - Recognize the complexity and uniqueness of individuals.

Remember, this is your journey. Understanding your personality type is just one tool to help you forge your path. The key to a meaningful career lies in understanding yourself and pursuing what truly resonates with you. Your personality type, interests, values, skills, and passions are all significant factors that, when considered together, can help guide you towards a satisfying and rewarding career.

We'll explore some common personality typologies and their relevance to career choices, followed by key guidelines and tips.

Different Personality Typologies

Myers-Briggs Type Indicator (MBTI): Extraversion/introversion, sensing/intuition, thinking/feeling, and judging/perceiving are the four dichotomies used by the MBTI to categorize people into 16 unique types.

For example, an ISTJ (introverted, sensing, thinking, judging) might thrive in a structured environment like accounting.

Holland Codes (RIASEC): People are classified into six personality types according to the RIASEC model: realistic, investigative, artistic, social, enterprising, and conventional.

For example, a person with an artistic personality might be drawn to creative careers such as design or writing.

DISC Personality Assessment: DISC measures four behavioural traits: dominance, influence, steadiness, and conscientiousness.

For example, someone with high dominance levels might excel in leadership roles.

Five-Factor Model (Big Five): Five major dimensions—openness, conscientiousness, extraversion, agreeableness, and neuroticism—are assessed by the Big Five.

For example, high conscientiousness may indicate a fit for careers requiring attention to detail and organization.

Another way of matching personality is exploring self-assessment tools.

Self-assessment tools are designed to measure various aspects of a person's personality, values, interests, and skills. These tools can offer insights into how a person might fit into specific careers, working environments, or roles.

Personality Assessments: Tools like the Myers-Briggs Type Indicator (MBTI), Holland Codes, DISC, and the Big Five can pinpoint personality traits and preferences.

Interest Inventories:

Assessments like the Strong Interest Inventory can help identify areas of interest pointing to specific careers.

Skills Assessments:

Tools that evaluate one's abilities and skills in certain areas provide insight into professions where those skills would be utilized.

Values Assessments:

Understanding personal values and how they align with various career paths is another valuable aspect of self-assessment.

Correlation between Specific Personality Types and Suitable Career Paths:

1. **Understanding Personality Typologies:**

a. Common personality models like the Myers-Briggs Type Indicator (MBTI), the Big Five, and the Holland Codes categorize individuals into different types or dimensions.

b. These models describe behavioural tendencies, motivations, interests, and values that influence how a person might thrive in various work environments.

2. **Identifying Career Alignments:**

a. Different personality types naturally align with certain professions or roles.
b. For example, an extroverted, sociable personality might thrive in sales or public relations, while an analytical, detail-oriented type might excel in fields like engineering or accounting.

3. **Applying Insights in Career Planning:**

a. Utilizing personality insights can help in career planning, job selection, educational choices, and personal development.

Strategies for Leveraging Personality Traits to Thrive in Chosen Careers:

Understanding Your Personality:

- Identify your core personality traits through self-reflection, Feedback, and possibly utilizing personality assessments.
- Recognize how these traits influence your working style, communication, decision-making, and collaboration.

Aligning Traits with Career Demands:

- Determine how your personality traits align or contrast with the demands and culture of your chosen career.
- Use your understanding to find roles, teams, and organizations where you will most likely excel.

Maximizing Strengths:

- Identify ways to apply your positive traits to excel in your job.
- For example, if you're naturally creative, look for opportunities to innovate and problem-solve within your role.

Mitigating Challenges:

- Recognize if any traits might create challenges in your chosen career and develop strategies to mitigate or overcome them.

Continuous Development:

- Understanding your personality and how it relates to your career should be an ongoing process. Continuously refine your strategies and expertise as you gain experience and grow.

> ### Key Guidelines to follow:
> - Choose Reputable Tools:
>   - Select scientifically validated and widely recognized assessments to ensure accurate and meaningful results.
> - Understand the Purpose:
>   - Be clear on what the assessment is meant to measure (e.g., personality, interests, skills) and how it can guide your career choices.
> - Take the Assessment Seriously:
>   - Provide honest and thoughtful responses to ensure the most accurate representation of your personality and preferences.
> - Interpret Results Carefully:
>   - If needed, seek guidance from career professionals to interpret and apply the results.

- Remember that no assessment can capture the full complexity of an individual.
- Integrate Multiple Perspectives:
    - Consider using a combination of assessments to comprehensively understand your personality, skills, interests, and values.
- Align With Career Exploration:
    - Use the insights from self-assessment tools to explore careers that align with your identified traits.
    - Research various professions, industries, and roles that match your profile.
- Reflect and Reassess:
    - Reflect on the results in the context of your experiences, goals, and intuition.
    - Periodically reassess as you grow and change to ensure ongoing alignment with your career path.
- Invest in Quality Assessments:
    - Use reputable and validated personality assessments to gain meaningful insights into personality types.
- Explore Various Models:
    - Different models might offer different perspectives; explore a few to get a well-rounded view.
- Consider the Whole Picture:
    - Personality is only one aspect of career fit. Consider other factors like skills, experience, and personal circumstances.
- Seek Professional Guidance:
    - Career counsellors or coaches who understand personality theory can provide personalized insights and guidance.

- Avoid Stereotyping:
  - While there are correlations, not every individual of a particular personality type will fit neatly into specific careers. Individual variation should be considered.
- Align With Personal Goals and Values:
  - Ensure that career choices align with personality and personal goals, values, and lifestyle preferences.
- Use as a Guideline, Not a Rule:
  - Personality insights are tools to guide career exploration, not definitive rules that dictate the "right" career.
- Continuously Reflect and Adapt:
  - People change and grow. Continuous reflection on personality alignment with career paths is valuable for ongoing satisfaction and success.
- Embrace Your Uniqueness:
  - Every personality has unique strengths and potential weaknesses. Embrace your individuality and use it to your advantage.
- Seek Feedback:
  - Regular feedback from colleagues and supervisors can provide insight into how your personality impacts your work.
- Adapt and Flex:
  - While leveraging your natural traits, also be willing to adapt and develop new skills as needed.
- Find the Right Fit:
  - If your personality significantly mismatches your current role, consider whether a different role or setting might be a better fit.

- Create a Personal Development Plan:
  - Based on your understanding of your personality, create a plan to develop the skills and behaviours needed to thrive in your chosen career.
- Use Mentors and Coaches:
  - Seek guidance from mentors or coaches who can provide personalized insights and help you develop strategies to leverage your personality effectively.
- Avoid Overemphasis on Personality Alone:
  - While personality is essential, don't overlook other factors like skills, experience, and external opportunities or challenges.
- Promote a Positive Workplace Environment:
  - Leverage your strengths to contribute to a positive, inclusive work environment where diverse personalities can thrive.

CHAPTER 1.6: CULTIVATING CURIOSITY AND PROBLEM-SOLVING SKILLS

Synopsis

Understanding Curiosity and Problem-Solving Skills

When flexed regularly, curiosity and problem-solving are cognitive muscles that can transform our approach to work and life. Curiosity is an innate interest in learning and understanding, exploring the unknown that leads to new discoveries. It's the fuel for innovation and creative thinking. Problem-solving, on the other hand, is a structured approach to address challenges and find solutions. It involves logic, creativity, resilience, and communication skills. Both these abilities are interlinked. While curiosity triggers questions and ignites the desire to learn, problem-solving allows us to use this acquired knowledge practically.

Example: Think of an inventor. Curiosity may spur them to understand why a particular device doesn't work as efficiently as it could. This curiosity, along with problem-solving skills, allows them to develop and create an improved version of the device.

The Role of Curiosity and Problem-Solving in Career Development

In a rapidly evolving employment market, the capability to learn new skills and adapt to change is vital. Curiosity drives lifelong learning, which is essential for career development in this ever-changing environment. On the other hand, problem-solving is a universally valued skill. Employers appreciate individuals who can navigate challenges effectively and produce solutions. Your curiosity might lead you to explore data visualization tools and techniques, addressing both the opportunity and threat. Your problem-solving skills will then enable you to learn these skills to overcome your weaknesses and ultimately leverage your strengths.

Example: A software developer's curiosity may drive them to explore the latest technologies or programming languages. Their problem-solving abilities will help them apply this new knowledge in troubleshooting or creating innovative software applications.

How to Cultivate Curiosity

Cultivating curiosity involves developing a mindset that embraces continuous learning and is open to new ideas. Start by asking questions about everything around you. Embrace a diverse range of topics, and don't be afraid to delve into unfamiliar territories.

- Create an 'I wonder' journal, where you jot down questions that spark your curiosity. Dedicate time to explore these questions and seek answers.
- Read one book per month outside your field.
- Engage in conversations with experts from different industries.
- Subscribe to podcasts or newsletters that offer a diverse range of topics.
- Solve puzzles or brain games regularly.
- Attend workshops or online courses on critical thinking.

- Engage in activities that require strategic planning (like chess or Sudoku)

How to Enhance Problem-Solving Skills

Improving problem-solving skills often involves developing certain sub-skills such as critical thinking, communication, creativity, and decision-making. It's about balancing analytical thinking and innovative, out-of-the-box ideas.

Practice problem-solving by challenging yourself with puzzles or brain teasers. You can also reflect on past problems you've encountered and consider different ways you might solve them now.

Balancing Curiosity and Problem-Solving

While curiosity encourages you to explore a breadth of knowledge, problem-solving requires a certain depth of knowledge to provide effective solutions. Balancing these two skills helps you to acquire a wide range of knowledge and apply it practically.

Example: A project manager, curious about improving team dynamics, may research various team-building techniques. By using their problem-solving skills, they could then devise a strategy using these techniques tailored to their team's unique challenges.

In summary, cultivating curiosity and problem-solving skills are pivotal for personal and professional growth. They can provide a competitive edge in your career, increase your adaptability, and lead to greater job satisfaction. Remember, the journey to develop these skills is iterative and continuous. So, stay inquisitive, embrace challenges, and never stop learning!

Cultivating curiosity and problem-solving skills can be incredibly beneficial in the realm of self-awareness. They help you expand your perspective, adapt to change, and seize opportunities that might not be evident to others. Let's dive in.

Practical Guide to Cultivating Curiosity and Problem-Solving Skills

Step 1: Embrace Curiosity

To cultivate curiosity, adopt a 'growth mindset'. Embrace every opportunity as a learning experience. Read extensively, engage in new activities, and converse with people from diverse backgrounds. Challenge and experiment with yourself to step out of your comfort zone.

For example, if you are in marketing, learn about design thinking, psychology, or data analysis. You open doors to innovative approaches and ideas in your field by broadening your knowledge horizon.

Step 2: Nurture Problem-Solving Skills

Problem-solving skills can be honed by practising structured thinking, analytical reasoning, and creative thinking. Participate in brainstorming sessions, engage in games that require strategic thinking, or take up courses on critical thinking.

Step 3: Integrate Curiosity and Problem-Solving

Curiosity asks the questions, and problem-solving provides the solutions. For instance, you might be curious about improving team productivity (the problem) and decide to learn about project management methodologies (the key).

Chapter 2

NAVIGATING OPPORTUNITY AWARENESS

Synopsis

At the intersection of ambition and achievement lies opportunity awareness. It's the active pursuit and recognition of possibilities within and beyond your current career path. An essential trait in today's fast-paced, dynamic job market, opportunity awareness can catalyse personal and professional growth. Much like a ship's compass in a vast and unpredictable ocean, opportunity awareness guides us toward uncharted territories in our professional lives. It's the skill of perceiving, comprehending, and seizing the chances that spring up along our career journey. Opportunity awareness can significantly determine your journey whether you're embarking on a fresh career path, climbing the corporate ladder, or contemplating a lateral move to broaden your professional scope.

1. Understanding Opportunity Awareness

Opportunity awareness is the conscious recognition and exploration of new chances for growth, be it in your existing role, within your organization, or in a broader professional landscape. It is not merely waiting for opportunities to present themselves but actively seeking them out. It's a multidimensional ability that spans comprehending industry trends, understanding shifts within organizations, evaluating areas for personal growth, and seeing where these elements intersect to yield unique career possibilities. It's like having a sixth sense tuned towards potential advancements on your professional path.

For instance, consider an IT professional. They might enhance their opportunity awareness by following technology trends, learning new programming languages, attending industry conferences, or networking with colleagues from different sectors. By doing so, they might discover an emerging field they're passionate about, perhaps AI or data science, opening doors for upskilling or even a career shift.

2. The Importance of Opportunity Awareness in Career Development

Opportunity awareness can significantly alter the trajectory of your career. By being tuned to potential opportunities, you put yourself in a position to grab them before they become apparent to others. It fosters adaptability, ensuring you stay relevant and desirable in a job market that's continually evolving.

Opportunity awareness forms a cornerstone in career development for several reasons:

a. Adaptability: With industries evolving rapidly, being aware of emerging trends, technologies, and fields allows you to adapt and remain relevant in your career.

b. Career Advancement: Recognizing and seizing the right opportunities can lead to promotions, project leads, or even job transitions that propel your career forward.

c. Professional Satisfaction: By being in tune with your professional landscape's opportunities, you're more likely to find roles or projects that align with your interests, leading to greater job satisfaction.

d. Risk Mitigation: Awareness of opportunities isn't only about advancement; it's also about recognizing potential threats to your career and proactively preparing or strategizing to mitigate those risks.

Practical Guide to Enhancing Opportunity Awareness includes:

Step 1: Broaden Your Horizons

Stay informed about industry trends and developments. Attend webinars, subscribe to relevant newsletters, and follow thought leaders in your field. For instance, a digital marketer might follow SEO trends and Google's algorithm updates.

Step 2: Network

Establish connections with people across different roles, departments, and organizations. Networking can reveal opportunities you might not discover independently.

Step 3: Seek Feedback and Mentorship

Regular feedback helps you recognize your strengths and areas for improvement. Mentorship provides a broader perspective and guidance on navigating your career landscape.

Step 4: Reflect and Strategize

Identify the types of opportunities that align with your career goals and devise strategies to pursue them. This step may involve upskilling, reskilling, or even job transitioning.

Step 5: Evaluate Personal and Professional Growth

Reflect on your skills and passions regularly. Are there areas you wish to improve? Or perhaps a new skill you want to learn? Consider how these align with your career goals.

Step 6: Connect the Dots

Merge your understanding of external trends with your personal and professional growth areas. Identify where they intersect to spot potential opportunities.

In conclusion, navigating opportunity awareness is about maintaining a 360-degree view of your career landscape, recognizing emerging possibilities, and strategically acting upon them. It's about steering your career, not just going with the flow. It's an empowering journey of exploration and growth that can enrich your career experience and propel you towards your desired professional milestones.

CHAPTER 2.1
FINDING WHAT'S BEST FOR YOU

Synopsis

The winding path of career development is an incredibly personal journey tied uniquely to each individual's skills, aspirations, experiences, and values. Unearthing what's best for you is a key ingredient in the recipe for a fulfilling career. It entails understanding one's interests, values, strengths, weaknesses, and aspirations and aligning these elements with a suitable career path. It is a critical part of the decision-making process that shapes the trajectory of your professional life, ensuring that you select a career that is not only rewarding but also fulfilling.

Recognizing the "best fit" for you does not follow a one-size-fits-all approach. Each individual's career is unique and shaped by their personal circumstances, values, skills, and aspirations. The key lies in the process of self-discovery and introspection that aids in mapping out the unique features of your personality, lifestyle preferences, and professional aspirations, which in turn determines the most suitable career paths.

1. What Does "Finding What's Best for You" Mean?

"Finding What's Best for You" means understanding yourself deeply – your strengths, weaknesses, passions, values, and how all of these pieces fit together to form your unique professional identity. It's about discerning which careers will provide personal satisfaction, motivate you to grow, and align with your life goals.

To illustrate, let's consider Alice, an extroverted individual with a knack for negotiation and a love for travel. Finding what's best for her might mean pursuing a career in international sales, where she can leverage her skills and passions while also fulfilling her desire to explore the world.

2. The Importance of Finding What's Best for You

Choosing a career path isn't merely about financial stability; it's about finding joy, purpose, and a sense of personal achievement. A career that aligns with your skills and passions will not only lead to higher job satisfaction but also inspire you to constantly improve and innovate, paving the way for long-term success and growth.

- **Promotes Job Satisfaction**: When your interests, values, and skills align with your career, you will likely enjoy your work, leading to higher job satisfaction and a more positive attitude.
- **Enhances Performance**: Individuals who are in careers that they consider a good fit are more likely to perform better. This is because they are doing what they love and are naturally inclined towards their work. They can leverage their strengths effectively, leading to enhanced productivity and success.
- **Boosts Career Longevity**: When you find what's best for you, you are less likely to experience burnout or consider frequent job changes. The satisfaction of doing what you love and excel at can contribute to a long, stable, and fulfilling career.

- **Contributes to Personal Growth**: Finding the best fit allows for the opportunity to grow and learn in areas that genuinely interest you, leading to a continuous personal and professional development cycle.
- **Leads to a Balanced Life**: When your career aligns with your personal values and lifestyle, it's easier to achieve a healthy work-life balance. You can meet your professional goals without sacrificing your individual needs and aspirations.

Imagine you're a creative person with a talent for drawing and a deep interest in technology. A graphic design career offers a platform for creativity and technology. In contrast, a data analyst position might offer excellent financial prospects but may not fulfil you, leading to disinterest and stagnation.

Guidelines for Finding What's Best for You

Finding what's best for you involves a process of self-discovery, exploration, and decision-making:

Step 1: Self-Discovery

Conduct a SWOT analysis, identify your passions and interests, understand your personality type, and define your values and life goals.

Step 2: Exploration

Research various industries, roles, and career paths. Look for fields where your skills and passions could be applied. Seek informational interviews or job shadowing opportunities to gain first-hand insight.

Step 3: Decision Making

Based on your self-discovery and exploration, shortlist careers that align with your aspirations. Consider factors like job availability, advancement opportunities, work-life balance, and remuneration.

Let's say you're a great communicator who loves storytelling but struggles with numerical analysis.

Ask this question to yourself!

What skills, experiences, or talents do I possess? The answer may be 'excellent communication skills' and 'a passion for storytelling.'

What areas need improvement or pose a challenge? For example, struggles with numerical analysis.

What careers align with my strengths and passions? I can have a career in public relations or content marketing.

What obstacles might hinder my path? Careers and areas requiring heavy data analysis might be challenging.

In summary, finding what's best for you involves a deep dive into self-understanding, thorough career exploration, and informed decision-making. It's about aligning who you are with what you do, creating a harmonious blend of personal satisfaction and professional accomplishment. Your perfect fit is out there; it's all about finding it.

CHAPTER 2.2: EXPLORING INTRIGUING INDUSTRIES AND FIELDS

Synopsis

Exploring intriguing industries and fields is fundamental to navigating opportunity awareness. It can be seen as a process of conducting research and gathering information about industries and professions that appeal to you. These explorations enable us to uncover potential career paths that align with our passions, skills, and life goals. It provides a broader perspective on the job market, allowing you to make informed career choices based on your skills, interests, and career aspirations. Moreover, it serves as a foundation for networking, skills development, and strategic career planning.

This exploration process involves gaining a comprehensive understanding of various sectors, their current market trends, potential growth, competitive landscape, and the available career opportunities. It also requires identifying the skills and qualifications needed to thrive in these fields. A thorough exploration allows you to determine the fit between you and your potential career, guiding you towards the right path and saving valuable time, energy, and resources.

1. What Does "Exploring Intriguing Industries and Fields" Mean?

Exploring intriguing industries and fields means researching and diving into various sectors of the professional world that catch your interest. This exploration can range from industries such as technology, healthcare, and finance to fields like environmental conservation, human rights, and the arts.

For instance, James, a computer science graduate interested in medicine, may explore the field of health informatics, combining both of his passions.

2. The Importance of Exploring Intriguing Industries and Fields

Understanding various industries and fields helps in informed decision-making about your career path. This exploration allows you to gain a broader perspective on available opportunities, providing a more accurate picture of where your skills and interests can best be utilized.

- **Informed Decision-Making**: Exploring industries and fields helps you make informed decisions about your career path. By understanding the dynamics of different sectors, you can select a path that aligns with your skills, interests, and career goals.
- **Skills and Knowledge Development**: This exploration process can reveal the essential skills and qualifications needed in specific fields, encouraging you to develop or acquire them to increase your employability.

- **Opportunity Identification**: It helps you identify new and emerging fields, thereby expanding your horizons and presenting opportunities you may not have considered before.
- **Networking**: Knowing more about different industries and fields can assist in expanding your professional network. It can guide you towards professionals, communities, and events related to your areas of interest.
- **Career Adaptability**: In today's rapidly changing job market, knowing various industries and fields enhances your adaptability. It prepares you for potential career shifts and contributes to career resilience.

Consider the example of Sarah, a creative writer with an interest in social causes. By exploring industries and fields, she discovers the realm of nonprofit communications, allowing her to use her writing skills to advocate for issues she's passionate about.

Guidelines for Exploring Intriguing Industries and Fields

Identifying Interests: Identify industries and fields that align with your skills, passions, and goals. Ask yourself: What relevant skills and experiences do you possess? What could hold you back in these fields?

Researching: Investigate these industries and fields, understanding their demands, opportunities, and trends. Try to figure out what trends or openings you can capitalize on. What obstacles or challenges could you encounter?

Networking: Connect with professionals in these fields to gain first-hand insight.

Experimenting: Internships, part-time jobs, or volunteering can provide valuable hands-on experience.

Exploring intriguing industries and fields is like charting a map of possibilities. It's a journey of discovery that uncovers various routes to your ultimate career destination. The more you explore, the more precise your path becomes. So, don't be afraid to dive deep, seek out new horizons, and embrace the adventure that leads to your future.

CHAPTER 2.3: SEEKING ADVICE FROM PROFESSIONALS

Synopsis

Professional guidance plays a substantial role in shaping careers. Seeking advice from professionals" is a process wherein individuals or entities solicit insights, recommendations, or guidance from trained or experienced individuals within a specific area of expertise. As we journey through our career paths, we might find ourselves at a crossroads, unsure of the best course of action. This is where professional advice comes into the picture, providing insights and recommendations based on knowledge, skills, and experience in a particular field. These professionals can be lawyers, doctors, financial advisors, engineers, psychologists, or any other persons possessing specialized knowledge, skills, and experience that average individuals may lack. This process can be crucial for decision-making, problem-solving, and achieving goals more efficiently and effectively.

Let's say you're considering transitioning from a career in technology to a career in management consulting. You could seek advice from professionals who have already made such transitions to understand the challenges and opportunities they encountered.

Professional advice is distinct from general advice in several ways. Firstly, professionals are usually certified or accredited by recognized bodies in their respective fields, ensuring high competency and adherence to specific ethical guidelines. They have dedicated years to rigorous training and study, keeping themselves updated with the latest research, theories, and trends in their field. Their advice is founded on a deep understanding of the subject matter.

Career counsellors, mentors, industry experts, or senior colleagues can guide you through the skills you need to acquire, the pros and cons of the transition, and even possible stepping stones. They can share their experiences, giving you real-world examples of what such a transition might look like, which can then inform your own decisions.

Secondly, professionals can often provide an unbiased viewpoint. They are detached from personal emotions and can see the bigger picture, thereby allowing them to make recommendations based on what is best for you or your situation. This contrasts with advice from friends or family members, which, while valuable, can sometimes be coloured by personal relationships or emotions.

Thirdly, when seeking professional advice, there is an element of liability. Professionals can be held accountable if they give faulty advice that leads to harm or loss. This increases the trustworthiness of professional advice because there is a higher level of responsibility for the advice given.

The importance of seeking advice from professionals can be seen in various aspects of life. Doctors, for example, can diagnose conditions and recommend treatments based on their comprehensive knowledge of the human body and diseases. In law, lawyers help interpret complicated legislation. They can represent or advise you in legal matters, helping to ensure your rights are protected. Financial advisors guide you in investment decisions, aiding in managing your financial resources to reach your financial goals.

In business, professional advice can be crucial for strategic decision-making and risk management. Business consultants may give insights into market trends, help develop effective marketing strategies, and optimize operational efficiency. This expert advice might spell the difference between the success or failure of a business.

In the personal realm, seeking professional advice is equally important. Mental health professionals can guide individuals through challenging times, providing strategies for managing stress, anxiety, and other emotional issues. Career counselors can assist individuals in making career decisions, aligning personal strengths and interests with career paths.

However, while the importance of seeking advice from professionals is evident, it's equally important to remember that professionals provide guidance, not decisions. At the end of the day, it's still up to the individual or organization to consider the advice, weigh the options, and make the final decision. Additionally, the quality of professional advice can vary, so it's wise to seek a second opinion if there are any doubts.

In conclusion, seeking advice from professionals refers to tapping into the knowledge and expertise of professionals across various fields. This advice is characterized by its basis in extensive training, impartiality, and liability. It plays an integral role in areas as diverse as medicine, law, finance, business, and personal development, empowering individuals and organizations to make informed decisions, solve complex problems, and ultimately achieve their goals more effectively.

Guides and Tips

- Research professionals in your field of interest: Use platforms like LinkedIn to identify professionals who have achieved success in your desired field or role.
- Ask the right questions: Instead of vague queries, ask specific questions. Instead of "How can I be successful?" ask, "What skills should I develop to thrive in this role?"
- Be proactive and respectful: Don't wait for professionals to approach you. However, remember to respect their time. Prepare beforehand to make the most of the interaction.
- Seek multiple viewpoints: Each professional will have a unique perspective. To gain a more rounded view, seek advice from various sources.

A few guidelines and tips to be handy are as follows:

1. Identify professionals
2. Research their background
3. Prepare specific questions
4. Request for meeting/appointment
5. Review and apply advice

6. Identify your career goals. Professionals can guide you on which opportunities are worth pursuing.
7. List your strengths
8. Identify your weak areas. Recognizing these areas can help you seek professional advice for improvement.
9. Find professionals who align with these goals
10. Be clear and respectful when seeking advice
11. Take notes and apply the advice
12. Keep the communication lines open for future guidance
13. Professionals can provide insights on navigating threats that can hinder achieving your goals

CHAPTER 2.4: NETWORKING TO CONNECT WITH LIKE-MINDED INDIVIDUALS

Synopsis

Networking to connect with like-minded individuals" plays a significant role in shaping our careers. This refers to the process of developing and nurturing relationships with people who share common interests, values, or goals. This form of networking involves establishing and nurturing relationships with people with similar interests, values, or professional objectives. Unlike generic networking, which focuses on the number of connections, networking with like-minded individuals prioritizes the quality of connections and shared experiences. This networking activity is often carried out at events, online communities, professional gatherings, or casual social meetups and is a key strategy for personal and professional growth.

Networking differs from regular socializing in its objective and structure. While all forms of socializing involve some level of interaction with others, networking is more strategic and purposeful. It aims to forge connections that can offer mutual benefits in the future, such as collaborations, partnerships, mentorship, or job opportunities.

Consider, for instance, an aspiring entrepreneur passionate about green technologies. By networking with individuals in this field, they can gain insights into industry trends, receive feedback on their ideas, possibly find a mentor, and even meet potential partners or investors. Networking, in this manner, becomes a pathway to opportunities otherwise unreachable.

This type of networking is distinct from the broader concept of networking, where the focus is on quantity—creating as many connections as possible, often for immediate benefits. When you network to connect with like-minded individuals, the emphasis is on the quality and depth of the relationship. You are not just looking for any connection; you are looking for connections with people who resonate with your values, passion, or ambition.

The importance of networking with like-minded individuals is manifold:

Shared Understanding: Like-minded individuals can relate to their experiences, challenges, and aspirations more deeply. They can provide advice that is more attuned to your specific situation, and their shared understanding can promote and provide a sense of community and belonging.

Motivation and Inspiration: Engaging with people who share your interests or goals can inspire and motivate you. Seeing others› success can drive you to strive harder, and sharing your journey can foster mutual encouragement.

Collaboration and Learning: Like-minded individuals often bring complementary skills or perspectives to the table. Collaboration can lead to innovation and growth. Moreover, these individuals can provide new knowledge or skills related to your shared interest, helping you learn and grow.

Career Opportunities: In professional settings, networking with like-minded individuals can open doors to job opportunities, partnerships, or business collaborations. These individuals can recommend you for roles that suit your interests and skills because they better understand your strengths and capabilities.

However, while the benefits are significant, one must approach this form of networking with authenticity and genuine interest. Relationships built on manipulation or self-serving interests tend to be short-lived and unfulfilling. Aim to offer value and support to others as much as you seek it for yourself.

In the age of digital technology, networking with like-minded individuals has become easier than ever. Social media platforms, online forums, and virtual events have made it possible to connect with people from all corners of the globe who share your interests. Remember, however, that networking is more than just connecting online; it involves nurturing these relationships over time through regular interactions and mutual support.

It must be followed as a strategic process of forging and nurturing relationships with individuals who share similar interests, values, or goals. Its focus is on the quality and depth of relationships rather than the sheer number of connections. Its importance lies in the shared understanding, motivation, collaboration, and career opportunities it offers; as with any form of networking, authenticity and genuine interest form the backbone of meaningful and lasting connections.

Guides and Tips

Identify your interests and values: Before networking, it's essential to understand what drives you, your interests, and your core values. Research and identify networking platforms. These factors will guide you to the right individuals and communities.

Choose the right platforms: Be it LinkedIn groups, industry forums, or local meetups, choose platforms where like-minded individuals gather. Initiate and maintain conversations and offer value and support.

Engage genuinely: Genuine engagement fosters stronger connections. Ask thoughtful questions, share valuable insights, and show genuine interest in others' viewpoints. Engaging actively and genuinely in nurturing relationships to continuously expand your network will recognize external factors you can use to your advantage.

Give before you take: Always look for ways to offer value to your connections. It could be sharing relevant resources, providing constructive feedback, or offering support in their projects.

Networking with like-minded individuals can aid your strengths and weaknesses. You may gain insights into opportunities and threats in the industry, or they may help you recognize your strengths and advise on mitigating weaknesses.

CHAPTER 2.5: EVALUATING TRANSFERABLE SKILLS IN DIFFERENT PROFESSIONS

Synopsis

A significant aspect of opportunity awareness is evaluating transferable skills in different professions. This is the process of identifying and assessing versatile and applicable skills across various job roles and industries that can be applied across multiple job roles and sectors, thus enhancing your adaptability in the job market. These skills, known as transferable skills, are valued highly by employers because of their broad applicability and their potential to boost productivity, enhance team dynamics, and facilitate problem-solving, among other benefits.

Transferable skills or talents can be either hard or soft skills or both. Hard skills are technical abilities learned through education, training, or experience, such as data analysis, project management, or proficiency in a foreign language. On the other hand, soft skills are related to your personality traits and include abilities such as communication, leadership, adaptability, and problem-solving.

Consider a career transition from teaching to corporate training. The ability to simplify complex concepts, public speaking skills, and understanding learning styles are all transferable skills that can be applied effectively in the new role.

While all skills are valuable, transferable skills have a unique advantage because of their versatility. Unlike job-specific skills relevant only within a particular role or industry, transferable skills apply to almost any job or profession. For example, a data analyst moving into a project management role may find that their analytical skills, attention to detail, and proficiency in data visualization tools are still relevant and beneficial in their new role.

Evaluating these skills is crucial for several reasons:

Career Transitions: Understanding your transferable skills can provide clarity during career transitions. It can help identify which roles you will likely excel in, even in a different industry, based on your existing skill set.

Job Applications: When applying for jobs, showcasing your transferable skills can increase your appeal to employers, particularly if you lack some job-specific skills.

Professional Development: Identifying your transferable skills can guide your professional development efforts. It can help you decide which skills to develop further and which new skills to learn.

Enhancing Performance: Understanding and leveraging your transferable skills can enhance your performance in your current role, even if those skills were developed in different positions or contexts.

However, evaluating transferable skills can be challenging because it requires introspection and looking beyond job titles and duties. It requires understanding the essence of what you do and how it can be applied in different contexts. Tools like skills assessment tests and career counselling can aid in this process.

Furthermore, recognizing your transferable skills is just the first step. You also need to communicate these skills effectively to potential employers. This means framing your experiences in a way that highlights the transferability of your skills, both in your resume and in job interviews.

In conclusion, evaluating transferable skills in different professions involves identifying and assessing versatile and widely applicable skills across job roles and industries. These transferable skills, both hard and soft, are valued for their broad applicability and potential to enhance productivity and team dynamics. Evaluating these skills is crucial for career transitions, job applications, professional development, and improving job performance. However, it requires introspection and looking beyond specific job roles, as well as the ability to communicate these skills effectively to potential employers.

Guides and Tips

Self-Assessment: Understanding your current skill set and identifying transferable skills. What are your most potent transferable skills? Review your past roles and experiences.

Identify the skills you used and how they could apply to other professions.

Research: Researching desired professions and matching skills into different occupations and the skills they demand. Which transferable skills do you lack or need to improve? Identify the overlap with your existing skills.

Showcase your transferable skills: When applying for jobs or discussing career transitions, highlight your transferable skills and give concrete examples of how you've used them.

Continuous Learning: Keep developing your transferable skills. This could be through new roles, professional courses, or self-learning.

In conclusion, evaluating transferable skills is integral to navigating opportunity awareness. By understanding your transferable skills, you can open new doors in your career, make smoother transitions, and stand out in the job market. Remember, skills are like tools in a toolbox—the more versatile your tools, the more tasks you can handle. Keep sharpening and adding to your skills, and you'll be better prepared to seize the opportunities that come your way.

Chapter 3

TAKING ACTION TOWARDS CAREER SUCCESS

Synopsis

As the ancient saying goes, a thousand-mile journey begins with one step. Taking action towards career success is about initiating this journey, steering through obstacles, and persistently moving towards your professional goals. It is about transforming dreams into reality.

Taking action towards career success is the proactive pursuit of goals and aspirations in one's professional life. It requires identifying career objectives, creating a strategic plan to reach them, and actively executing this plan. This process is central to achieving professional growth and long-term success in any field.

Taking action is different from merely having career goals or aspirations. Many people have ambitions, but those who achieve success are those who take decisive steps to realize these ambitions. For instance, an individual might aspire to become a top-level manager in a multinational corporation. However, this goal will remain an unfulfilled dream unless they seek relevant education, gain professional experience, network with industry professionals, develop leadership skills, and continuously learn and adapt.

Furthermore, taking action towards career success is also distinct from routine job activities. While day-to-day tasks are essential for maintaining performance, they may not necessarily lead to significant professional growth or success. This often requires extra actions, such as taking on challenging projects, seeking constructive feedback, investing in professional development, or stepping out of the comfort zone to seize new opportunities.

The importance of taking action towards career success cannot be overstated:

Set Clear Goals: Understand what you want to achieve in your career. Ensure your goals and objectives are specific, measurable, achievable, relevant, and time-bound (SMART).

Achieving Goals: Taking action bridges career goals and their achievement. Without action, goals remain mere wishes.

Create a Plan: Outline a detailed plan to reach your goals. Break it down into small, manageable steps.

Personal Growth: The process of taking action involves learning, overcoming challenges, and stepping out of comfort zones. This leads to personal growth and development.

Take the Initiative:

1. Don't wait for opportunities to come your way.
2. Seek them out.
3. Initiate projects, engage in networking, and apply for that job or promotion.

Increased Job Satisfaction: Actively working towards career success often leads to increased job satisfaction. It makes the work more meaningful and fulfilling.

Career Advancement: Taking action can lead to significant career advancements, such as promotions, increased salary, or recognition.

Greater Opportunities: By proactively working towards career success, individuals can open up new opportunities that may have been otherwise inaccessible.

Persevere: The road to success is not always smooth. There will be setbacks. Don't let them deter you. Stay committed to your goals.

Never Stop Learning: Continually enhance your skills and knowledge. Attend workshops, take courses, and read widely.

Stay Adaptable: Be prepared to adjust your plan as circumstances change. The job market and industry trends can shift. Stay flexible.

The process of taking action towards career success involves several steps, including goal setting, planning, taking Initiative, perseverance, continuous learning, and adaptability. Each step is critical and contributes to the overall journey towards career success.

For example, goal setting provides a direction, planning outlines the path to reach the goal, taking Initiative involves starting the journey and making active efforts, perseverance is about maintaining the efforts despite challenges, continuous learning helps adapt to changes and improve skills, and adaptability allows for adjusting the plans and actions based on changing circumstances or opportunities.

> **Key points to remember**
> - Identify your strong points that can help you in achieving your career goals
> - Setting clear career goals
> - Clear and SMART goals
> - Understand your weaknesses that might hinder your progress
> - Prepare a detailed action plan
> - Initiative and proactive actions
> - Acknowledge potential challenges. Perseverance in the face of challenges
> - Creating and executing an action plan
> - Taking initiative in professional pursuits
> - Staying committed and resilient
> - Continuously updating skills and knowledge
> - Staying adaptable to changing circumstances

In conclusion, taking action towards career success is about more than merely dreaming of success. It's about making it happen by creating a strategic plan to achieve it and actively implementing this plan. It is critical for realizing professional aspirations, personal growth, increased job satisfaction, career advancement, and opening up new opportunities. The process requires goal setting, planning, Initiative, perseverance, continuous learning, and adaptability, each contributing to the overall journey towards career success. Whether you're an aspiring novelist, a hopeful entrepreneur, or a professional aiming for the top, remember that your actions turn your professional aspirations into reality. So, set your goals, craft your plan, take that first step, and embark on your journey to success.

CHAPTER 3.1: IDENTIFYING AND OVERCOMING BARRIERS

Synopsis

In our career journeys, we often encounter barriers that impede our progress. If not adequately addressed, these barriers can derail our pursuit of career success. Hence, identifying and overcoming these barriers is key to taking action towards career success.

Identifying and overcoming barriers is critical in personal and professional development. It involves recognizing obstacles that hinder progress and finding effective solutions to mitigate or eliminate their impact. These barriers could be internal, such as fears, insecurities, or lack of skills, or external, such as financial constraints, societal norms, or lack of opportunities.

The process starts with identification, which requires self-awareness, introspection, and sometimes external feedback. It involves understanding the nature of the barrier and how it obstructs progress. For example, a person aspiring to be a public speaker may recognize their fear of public speaking as a barrier. I still remember having shivers and would choose to hide myself so that I would not be called on stage for any performance, speech, etc. However, I used to participate with a lot of push from my parents and teachers in group dramas. However, individual performance was a big challenge for me for a long time until I startered was in engineering college. Similarly, an individual wanting to start a business may identify a lack of capital as an external barrier.

Overcoming barriers, on the other hand, involves finding ways to navigate or remove these obstacles. It requires problem-solving, resilience, creativity, and sometimes external help or resources. Following the previous examples, the aspiring public speaker might join a local Toastmasters club to overcome their fear. In contrast, the aspiring entrepreneur might seek investors or take a loan to overcome their financial constraints. I am sharing my story here. As I have a passion for listening to and singing music, I got few opportunities to showcase my talent. But as there was fear in the back of my mind, my passion for music and singing made me overcome the fear, and I stood on stage and sang on multiple occasions. Thus, you have to identify the barrier and work on it with your passion and interest involved to eliminate and overcome it.

Imagine you're a salesperson with an ambition to lead a team, but you grapple with public speaking anxiety. This fear is a barrier, preventing you from demonstrating leadership skills and climbing the career ladder.

Identifying and overcoming barriers is of immense importance for several reasons:

Achievement of Goals: Barriers, by definition, obstruct progress towards goals. Therefore, identifying and overcoming them is essential for achieving personal or professional goals.

Personal Growth: Dealing with barriers often leads to learning, growth, and development. For example, overcoming fear can increase confidence, while finding ways to gather resources can enhance problem-solving skills.

Empowerment: Successfully overcoming a barrier can be empowering. It boosts self-efficacy, the belief in one's ability to succeed, which further aids in tackling future obstacles.

Improved Well-being: Barriers often cause stress and frustration. Overcoming them can improve mental and emotional well-being.

Unlocking Potential: Sometimes, barriers keep people stuck in their comfort zones, limiting their potential. Overcoming these barriers can unlock new possibilities, opportunities, and achievements.

However, it's crucial to remember that identifying and overcoming barriers is not always a straightforward process. It often requires patience, persistence, and a willingness to step out of one's comfort zone. Some barriers may also require professional help to overcome, such as mental health issues or deep-seated fears. Lastly, it's essential to view barriers not just as obstacles but as opportunities for growth and learning.

Guides and Tips
Identify Your Barriers:

1. Spend time reflecting on your *fears, insecurities, and limitations*.
2. Identify what are your weaknesses or barriers.

3. Analyze what are your strengths that can help you overcome barriers.
4. Recognize any external factors like lack of opportunities or resources that might be impeding your progress.

Seek Feedback: Feedback from colleagues, mentors, or coaches can provide valuable insights into potential barriers you might not be aware of.

Devise a Strategy: Once you've identified your barriers, create an action plan to overcome them. What are the opportunities that can help you tackle your barriers? This could involve seeking additional training, practising a skill, or seeking professional help.

Persistence: Overcoming barriers often takes time and repeated efforts. Don't get disheartened by initial setbacks. Remember, every step, no matter how small, brings you closer to your goal.

Seek Support: You don't have to face your barriers alone. Seek support from mentors, peers, or professionals. They can provide guidance, resources, and encouragement.

By analysis, you can design effective strategies to leverage your strengths and opportunities, improve your weaknesses, and mitigate threats. This way, our salesperson could enrol in public speaking workshops (leveraging opportunities), practice presentations with their team (utilizing strengths), and gradually reduce their anxiety (improving weakness), all while maintaining a positive mindset to combat the competitive pressure (mitigating threats).

In conclusion, identifying and overcoming barriers is an integral part of taking action towards career success in personal and professional development that involves recognizing and tackling obstacles to progress. It's about understanding your fears and limitations, devising a strategy to tackle them, and persistently moving forward. Each barrier overcome is a victory, a step closer to your career success. It is essential for achieving goals, personal growth, empowerment, improved well-being, and unlocking potential.

Remember, it's not the absence of barriers that sets successful people apart; it's their determination to overcome them. So, face your obstacles, embrace the challenge, and confidently advance your career goals. While it can be challenging, the rewards make it a worthwhile endeavour.

CHAPTER 3.2: BRIDGING THE GAP WITH RELEVANT EDUCATION OR EXPERIENCE

Synopsis

In the course of our career journey, we may encounter the inevitable "skill gap," a mismatch between the skills we currently possess and the skills required for a career move or advancement. Bridging this gap with relevant education or experience is a pivotal step towards career success. Bridging the gap with relevant education or experience is a proactive strategy that involves understanding the difference between one's current skills, knowledge, or abilities and what is required for a specific goal and then undertaking necessary learning or gaining appropriate experiences to fulfil these requirements. This process can be applied in various contexts, most commonly in career development, where individuals strive to close the gap between their current capabilities and the requirements of a desired role or profession.

Bridging the gap differs from traditional learning or professional development in its focus and purpose. Traditional learning is often broad-based, focusing on acquiring a wide variety of knowledge, information and skills, while professional development usually aims to enhance one's skills within a current role. However, bridging the gap is more targeted. It involves identifying specific skill gaps related to a particular goal and then seeking education or experiences to address these gaps.

For example, a software engineer aspiring to become a data scientist would need to bridge the gap in their knowledge of data science principles, tools, and techniques, which could be accomplished through targeted courses, boot camps, or hands-on projects.

Consider this scenario: Sarah, a marketing manager, wants to move into the thriving field of digital marketing. However, she has little experience in SEO and social media strategies. Sarah identifies this skill gap and takes action to bridge it by going through relevant courses and understanding to enhance her skill set. Sarah lacks in-depth knowledge and experience in digital marketing, thus strengthening and bridging the gap.

This process is vital for several reasons:

Career Progression: It enables individuals to acquire the necessary skills or experience to advance in their careers, transition to new roles, or enter new fields.

Professional Competence: It helps maintain and enhance professional competence by ensuring individuals have the most relevant and up-to-date skills.

Competitive Advantage: It gives individuals a competitive edge in the job market by demonstrating a proactive approach to learning and adaptability to changing job requirements.

Personal Growth: It contributes to personal growth and confidence as individuals expand their skill sets and face new challenges.

Job Satisfaction: It can lead to lead to increased job reverted to satisfaction as individuals feel more competent and empowered in their roles.

Guides and Tips

Identify Your Skill Gap: Understand the requirements of your career goal and compare them with your current skills and experiences.

Acquire Relevant Education: Seek educational opportunities that can help you acquire the needed skills. Potential options include online courses, boot camps, certifications, or even a degree program.

Gain Relevant Experience: Seek opportunities to gain hands-on experience. Volunteering, internships, projects, or even taking on related tasks in your current job can provide valuable experience.

Showcase Your New Skills: Update your resume, LinkedIn profile, or portfolio to reflect your new skills and experiences.

Keep Learning: Skill requirements evolve with time. Continuous learning is the key and vital for staying relevant in your career.

Key points to remember and follow:

- Understanding your skill gap
- Identifying education opportunities and acquiring relevant education
- Seeking experiences to apply new skills. What resources or opportunities are available for you to learn and gain experience? For example, Sarah could leverage online courses, webinars, or digital marketing projects in her company.
- Showcasing acquired skills and your new skills
- Commitment to lifelong learning

In conclusion, bridging the gap with relevant education or experience is a focused and purposeful approach to personal and professional development. It is a decisive step towards career success. It involves identifying specific skill gaps related to a goal and seeking targeted education or experiences to address these gaps and taking a proactive approach to identify your skill gaps, seek targeted education, gain relevant experience, and consistently adapt to the evolving requirements of your career path. With each gap you bridge, you unlock a new level of capability, bringing you closer to your career aspirations. It is essential for career progression, maintaining professional competence, gaining a competitive advantage, personal growth, and increased job satisfaction.

The process can be challenging and require significant commitment. However, it is ultimately rewarding as it empowers and allows individuals to achieve their goals and realize their full potential. Remember, in the journey of career success, those who continuously learn and adapt are the ones who thrive.

CHAPTER 3.3: MANAGING TIME AND OVERCOMING PROCRASTINATION

Synopsis

A seamless flow of productivity can often be hindered by two major roadblocks: poor time management and procrastination. These two interconnected yet distinct concepts can significantly influence our career trajectories. Managing time and overcoming procrastination is about effectively organizing one's time and tasks while simultaneously combating the habit of postponing tasks that need to be accomplished. These two concepts, though interconnected, address distinct facets of productivity and efficiency.

Time management is the ability to plan and control how one spends the hours in a day to effectively accomplish their goals. It is the practice of allocating one›s time to tasks and projects based on their priority and urgency. This includes setting goals, prioritizing tasks, planning, scheduling, and organizing tasks to maximize efficiency and productivity. Effective time management allows individuals to get more done in less time, reduces stress, improves focus, increases opportunities for learning and development, and ultimately leads to better career success and personal fulfilment.

On the other hand, overcoming **procrastination**—often viewed as the thief of time—focuses on addressing the habit of delaying tasks that should be done immediately. Procrastination is a complex issue, often stemming from factors like fear of failure, decision fatigue, perfectionism, or lack of motivation.

Overcoming procrastination involves:

- Recognizing and understanding why you procrastinate.
- Creating a conducive environment.
- Breaking tasks into smaller parts.
- Setting realistic goals.
- Rewarding oneself upon task completion.

Time management and overcoming procrastination are fundamentally different. The former is a positive action towards goal completion, whereas the latter is often seen as a barrier to productivity. However, they are intimately connected since effective time management can help combat procrastination. Though both focus on improving productivity, time management emphasizes the 'when' and 'how' of accomplishing tasks, while overcoming procrastination tackles the 'why' behind task delay.

The importance of these skills is multifold.

Improves Productivity: Effective time management allows for increased productivity by enabling you to complete tasks within set deadlines. Similarly, overcoming procrastination removes unnecessary delays, ensuring work gets done on time. By managing time effectively and overcoming procrastination, you can accomplish more in a given time frame, thus boosting productivity.

Reduces Stress: Managing time reduces the stress associated with last-minute tasks or missed deadlines. Overcoming procrastination, too, helps eliminate the anxiety and guilt associated with putting off jobs. Knowing what needs to be done and when reduces the stress related to workload and deadlines. It gives you control over your tasks and time.

Enhances Quality of Work/ Professional Reputation: Effective time managers are seen as reliable and competent, enhancing their professional reputation. Overcoming procrastination improves others' perception of you, showing that you're proactive and diligent. With adequate time to complete tasks, the quality of work improves. It also allows for time to review and improve the work further.

Facilitates Career Advancement: Effective time management skills are highly regarded in the workplace and can significantly aid career advancement. Similarly, those who overcome procrastination are often more likely to take on new challenges and opportunities. Individuals who consistently meet deadlines are more likely to receive recognition and promotions.

Balances Work and Personal Life: Good time management can help you and also contribute to a healthier work-life balance, allowing for dedicated time for relaxation and personal pursuits. By overcoming procrastination, you can ensure tasks don't spill over into your personal time.

Boosts Confidence and Self-Esteem: Successfully managing tasks and overcoming procrastination enhances self-confidence and creates a positive productivity loop.

Imagine John, a talented software developer who aspires to move into a project management role. Despite his talent, John struggles with time management and often procrastinates on tasks. As a result, he finds it challenging to prepare for the transition to his desired role.

Guides and Tips

Set SMART Goals: Specific, measurable, achievable, relevant, and time-bound goals provide a clear direction for your time and effort.

Tasks Prioritization: Not all tasks are created equal. Use the Eisenhower Box (Urgent-Important Matrix) to prioritize tasks based on urgency and importance.

Create a Schedule: Dedicate specific time blocks for different tasks. Consider your energy levels at other times of the day.

Break Down Tasks: Large tasks can seem daunting. Break things down into smaller, manageable tasks to reduce the urge to procrastinate.

Eliminate Distractions: Identify and eliminate or reduce anything that distracts you from focusing on tasks.

Practice Mindfulness: Stay present and focused on the task at hand. This reduces the tendency to delay tasks.

> **Key points to consider**
>
> 1. Understanding the importance of time management and overcoming procrastination. What time management skills do you already possess?
> 2. Identifying your time management techniques and strategies to overcome procrastination. What makes you procrastinate or mismanage your time?
> 3. Planning and scheduling tasks. What could hinder your time management and encourage procrastination?
> 4. Prioritizing tasks based on urgency and importance. What resources or methods can you use to improve?
> 5. Staying focused and mindful.

In conclusion, managing time and overcoming procrastination are key skills significantly impacting personal and professional life. They address different aspects of productivity—when and how to do tasks versus why tasks are being delayed. Time management and overcoming procrastination are essential steps towards career success. They offer a way to harness your most valuable resource, time, by focusing on goal setting, task prioritization, scheduling, and creating a conducive environment for work. While it may take time and consistent effort to master these skills, the payoff is enormous in terms of productivity, work quality, career growth, and overall life satisfaction. Combining effective time management strategies and tactics to overcome procrastination can improve productivity, better work quality, career growth, and a more balanced and satisfying life.

CHAPTER 3.4: EMBRACING FINANCIAL RESPONSIBILITY

Synopsis

As we embark on our career journey, we often focus solely on enhancing our skills, gaining experiences, and seeking promotions. However, alongside these factors, embracing financial responsibility is another crucial aspect that plays an instrumental role in career success. Embracing financial responsibility refers to consciously accepting and effectively managing one's financial affairs. It entails understanding and managing your financial resources effectively to ensure stability, independence, and long-term success. This concept revolves around being accountable for one's financial decisions, spending habits, savings, and overall financial well-being.

Financial responsibility involves various actions and decisions, including saving, budgeting, investing, and managing debt. It's not just about earning money but using it wisely to secure your present and future. This concept goes beyond individual gains as it influences the economy at large. A financially responsible workforce is likely to make prudent decisions, driving economic growth and stability.

There are three key components to financial responsibility.

Budgeting and Saving: Budgeting involves planning your income and expenses, ensuring you live within your means, and saving a part of your income for future needs or emergencies. It's about controlling your money instead of letting it control you. Regular saving is crucial for both short-term needs (like vacations or gadgets) and long-term goals (like retirement or a home purchase).

Debt Management: Financial responsibility requires you to manage and reduce debts effectively. Understanding the terms of your debts, making timely payments, and strategizing to pay off debts early can contribute to a healthier financial life.

Investing: Investing wisely is a key to wealth creation and financial security. It involves understanding various investment options, assessing your risk tolerance, and building a diversified investment portfolio.

Differences Between Budgeting, Debt Management, and Investing

Understanding the differences between budgeting, debt management, and investing is vital to financial responsibility.

Budgeting is creating a plan to spend your money, allowing you to decide in advance whether you'll have enough money for the things you need or would like to do. This involves planning how to spend money, including allocating funds for necessities, discretionary items, savings, and emergencies.

Debt management, on the other hand, is about controlling and reducing the money you owe to others, either through better planning, reducing spending, or renegotiating payment terms.

Investing is allocating/assigning resources, generally money, with the expectation and goal of generating an income or profit. Money saved can be invested to grow over time. This could involve stocks, bonds, real estate, mutual funds, or retirement accounts. This still needs careful study and understanding and can't be done in haste for the sake of investing.

Importance of Embracing Financial Responsibility in Shaping Your Career

Career Flexibility: Being financially responsible allows you to make career decisions based on your interests and passions rather than financial pressures. You can explore different industries or fields or even start your own business.

Personal Stability: Financial stability ensures personal stability. It gives you peace of mind, allowing you to focus on your job and perform better.

Career Progression: Understanding financial concepts can help in career progression, especially if you aspire to climb the corporate ladder. It is crucial in budgeting, resource allocation, and strategic decision-making.

Retirement Planning: Financial responsibility includes planning for your retirement. Starting early can lead to a comfortable and secure retirement.

Avoiding Unnecessary Debt: While some debt may be unavoidable (like a mortgage or student loan), accumulating unnecessary debt (like credit card debt from impulse purchases) can be detrimental.

Planning for the Future: Embracing financial responsibility includes planning for the future. This includes setting financial goals, planning for retirement, and ensuring you're financially prepared for unexpected situations. This might involve saving for retirement, investing to grow wealth, or setting financial goals.

Financial Security: Responsible financial habits lead to financial security and independence. This includes having savings for emergencies, being able to afford necessities, and having funds for future goals.

Reduced Stress: Financial problems are a common source of stress. Financial responsibility helps mitigate these worries by ensuring you're prepared for unexpected expenses and living within your means.

Freedom and Flexibility: When you're financially responsible, you have more freedom to make choices that align with your personal and professional goals. This could include changing careers, starting a business, or pursuing further education.

Legacy: By managing your finances responsibly, you can leave a legacy for your children or grandchildren. This could include financial assets or a strong example of financial responsibility.

Let's take the example of Laura, a young marketing executive. Despite earning a good salary, Laura lives paycheck to paycheck, with little saved for the future or unexpected emergencies.

Guides and Tips

Create a Budget: Starts with listing your income and expenses. This clarifies where your money is going and where you can make adjustments.

Start Saving: Even if it's a small amount, start saving regularly. Aim for an emergency fund capable of covering 3-6 months of living expenses.

Invest Wisely: Make your money work for you. Explore safe and reliable investment avenues to grow your savings.

Avoid Unnecessary Debt: Use credit cards judiciously and avoid high-interest loans.

Plan for Retirement: It's never too early to start. Consider contributing to a retirement fund from the early stages of your career.

Key Points to Consider

- Understand the importance of financial responsibility
- Learn how to develop a budget and stick to it
- Discover ways to save and invest wisely
- Know how to manage and avoid unnecessary debt
- Begin planning for retirement
- Ask and analyze what financial skills or habits you already possess
- Identify what financial habits need improvement
- Define objectives to know what resources or strategies can improve your financial health

It is vital to know that obstacles could hinder your financial stability and to be prepared for it.

Embracing financial responsibility is an essential step towards personal and career success. It's not just about earning more money but also about how you manage, save, and grow that money. By developing sound financial habits like budgeting, saving, investing wisely, and avoiding unnecessary debt, you can achieve financial stability and security, reduce stress, plan for the future, and have more freedom and flexibility in your personal and professional life. It is about accepting and managing one's financial affairs effectively. The importance of embracing financial responsibility is profound, leading to financial security, reduced stress, future planning, freedom, flexibility, and the potential to leave a legacy. It's a crucial life skill that everyone should strive to master.

CHAPTER 3.5: OVERCOMING THE FEAR OF FAILURE

Synopsis

In the arena of career progression, one obstacle often stands as a formidable foe—the fear of failure. If left unaddressed, this fear can immobilize us, restricting us from seizing opportunities and reaching our full potential. It's important to understand that failure is not the end of the journey but a stepping-stone to learning, growth, and success. Fear of failure must be transformed into a positive driving force, enabling us to take calculated risks, seek new opportunities, and strive for success.

Overcoming the fear of failure" refers to conquering the apprehension or anxiety that arises from the possibility of not succeeding in a task or goal. This fear can often be crippling, hindering individuals from taking risks or attempting new ventures, both in personal and professional contexts.

The fear of failure, also known as atychiphobia, can manifest itself in various ways. Some people might procrastinate, delay decisions, or avoid challenging tasks to evade the risk of failure. Others might over-prepare or become perfectionistic to minimize the chance of failing.

Understanding and overcoming the fear of failure involves four key steps:

Recognition: Identify and acknowledge your fear of failure. Understanding your fears and their sources can help you address them effectively.

Rationalization: Challenge the irrational beliefs associated with your fear. Remember, everyone makes mistakes, and it's through these mistakes that we learn and grow.

Resilience: Develop emotional resilience. Treat setbacks as opportunities for learning rather than reflecting your abilities or self-worth.

Reorientation: Cultivate a growth mindset, viewing failure as a stepping stone towards success.

Let's take a deeper look into these steps.

Recognition is the first step towards overcoming the fear of failure. It involves acknowledging your fears and understanding their origin. Fear often stems from negative past experiences or the unrealistic expectations set by oneself or others. By recognizing these fears, you pave the way towards addressing them constructively.

Rationalization involves confronting and challenging irrational fears and beliefs about failure. Realize that failure is a part of life and that everyone eventually fails. What matters is not the failure itself but how you respond to it.

Resilience, in simple terms, can be said is the ability to bounce back and recover from setbacks. It's about developing the emotional strength to handle and recover from challenges swiftly. Building resilience can involve various strategies, including positive self-talk, maintaining a support network, and practising stress management techniques.

Reorientation is about adopting a growth mindset - a belief system that views challenges as opportunities for learning and growth rather than threats. People with a growth mindset view failure not as evidence of unintelligence or incapability but as a catalyst for stretching existing abilities and mastering new ones.

Importance of Overcoming Fear of Failure in Shaping Your Career

Fosters Risk-Taking: Overcoming the fear of failure encourages risk-taking, a vital component of career growth and success. It enables you to step out beyond your comfort zone and seize opportunities.

Promotes Learning: Each failure provides a unique learning opportunity. Embracing failure allows you to learn from your mistakes and continuously improve.

Drives Innovation: Innovation often requires trial and error. By conquering your fear of failure, you can cultivate an environment of innovation and creativity in your career.

Improves Decision-Making: When you're not inhibited by the fear of failure, you can make decisions more confidently and objectively.

Enhances Resilience: Each encounter with failure enhances your resilience, preparing you to face future challenges more effectively. However, failure, when approached healthily, is a powerful learning tool. It provides invaluable lessons, fosters resilience, and can be the stepping-stone to eventual success. Therefore, overcoming the fear of failure is not about avoiding failure altogether but about reframing and understanding failure from a different perspective.

The process of overcoming the fear of failure involves several key steps:

Recognize the Fear: Recognize that the fear of failure exists and it's a normal part of being human. Recognizing the presence of failure is the first step towards overcoming it.

Reframe Failure: See failure as an opportunity to learn and grow rather than a devastating end. Understand failure as an opportunity for growth. Remember that every mistake has a lesson embedded within it.

Set Realistic Goals: Setting unattainable goals can amplify the fear of failure. Aim for achievable goals that encourage growth without inciting overwhelming fear. Ambitious goals are good, but they should be attainable. Unrealistic goals may increase the fear of failure.

Practice Self-Compassion: Be kind to yourself when you experience failure. It's an integral part of life and does not define your worth. You are more than the sum of your failures and successes.

Seek Support: If the fear of failure becomes too much to bear, consider seeking support from a mental health professional, a mentor, a peer, or a professional counsellor.

The significance of conquering the fear of failure is vast.

Personal Growth: When the fear of failure does not hold you back, you're more likely to take risks and explore new possibilities, leading to personal growth.

Resilience: Overcoming fear of failure helps build resilience, the ability to bounce back from setbacks.

Success: By not fearing failure, you increase your chances of success. Many of the world's most successful people have experienced numerous failures along their journey.

Innovation: Fear of failure stifles creativity and innovation. By overcoming this fear, you can foster a more innovative mindset, which benefits any career or life path.

Happiness and Satisfaction: Living in constant fear of failure can lead to stress and unhappiness. Overcoming this fear can lead to increased satisfaction and joy in life.

> **Key points to remember and follow:**
> - Recognize and acknowledge the fear of failure
> - Identify what qualities give you strength in the face of failure.

- Understand the areas that fuel your fear of failure and what challenges could amplify your fear of failure
- Understand the process of reframing failure.
- Look for resources or strategies that could help you overcome your fear
- Learn to set achievable goals
- Cultivate and practice self-compassion in times of failure
- Seek support when needed.

Overcoming the fear of failure involves reframing our perception of failure and understanding it as a catalyst for learning, resilience, and eventual success. This process is crucial for personal and professional growth success, fostering innovation, and improving overall happiness and life satisfaction. Overcoming the fear of failure is not only about avoiding adverse outcomes but more about harnessing failure as a stepping stone for growth and success. Recognizing fear, reframing failure, setting realistic goals, practising self-compassion, and seeking help when needed are critical steps towards conquering the fear of failure. By mastering these steps, you can bolster your resilience, nurture your personal growth, unlock success, stimulate innovation, and enjoy a happier, more fulfilling career.

CHAPTER 3.6: BUILDING EMOTIONAL RESILIENCE

Synopsis

During our professional journey, we often confront challenges and setbacks. It's the strength of our emotional resilience that determines not just our ability to bounce back but also to grow and thrive in the face of adversity. Emotional resilience refers to one's ability to adapt to stressful situations or crises. Resilient individuals can 'roll with the punches,' bouncing back from challenges and adversity more effectively and swiftly. Building emotional resilience refers to developing the capacity to withstand, adapt to, and recover from adversity, stress, and life's challenges.

Emotional resilience is not about avoiding hardships or sidestepping difficulties but rather about learning to cope effectively with them, maintaining emotional balance, and bouncing back more robustly. People with strong emotional resilience don't let failure define them; instead, they use the experience to grow and improve. This ability is not about pretending everything is fine but about being optimistic and proactive in facing difficulty.

Building emotional resilience involves enhancing your capacity to handle pressure and stress, manage emotions, navigate adversity, recover from setbacks, and adapt to change. It's about cultivating a mindset that can help you maintain balance in your life, even during challenging times.

Emotional resilience can vary significantly from person to person. For some, resilience might mean the ability to keep composed under high stress, while for others, it might mean the capacity to bounce back after a significant setback or loss. However, regardless of how it manifests, the core of emotional resilience lies in the ability to navigate hardship with strength and flexibility.

The importance of building emotional resilience cannot be overstated.

Promotes Stress Management: Emotional resilience aids in managing and reducing stress, preventing burnout, and maintaining mental health.

Healthy Relationships: Resilience can improve relationships by encouraging empathy, effective communication, and conflict-resolution skills.

Fosters Adaptability: The corporate world is dynamic and ever-changing. Employees often face new challenges and disruptions, such as changing roles, layoffs, restructuring, or new technology. Emotional resilience enables individuals to adapt to these changes with minimal disruption. Emotional resilience fosters adaptability, allowing individuals to cope with change effectively, a crucial ability in our ever-changing world.

Career Success: Companies value emotionally resilient employees as they are reliable under pressure, efficient problem solvers, and effective leaders. These qualities can significantly contribute to career advancement. Resilience can lead to better job performance, improved problem-solving skills, and increased job satisfaction.

Enhances Problem-Solving Skills: Building emotional resilience enhances your problem-solving and decision-making abilities. It encourages a proactive approach, where you perceive challenges as opportunities rather than threats.

Facilitates Recovery from Setbacks: Failure and setbacks are inevitable in any career journey. Resilient individuals can recover from these setbacks quickly and effectively. They see failures as learning opportunities and use them to fuel future success.

Supports Professional Relationships: Resilient people can handle interpersonal challenges in the workplace better. They can manage conflict, offer support to colleagues, and maintain positive relationships, even in stressful situations.

Overall Well-being: Building emotional resilience increases happiness, life satisfaction, and overall well-being.

Building emotional resilience involves several vital strategies:

Mindfulness: Practicing mindfulness helps acknowledge and accept feelings, contributing to resilience.

Self-care: Taking care of physical health can improve emotional resilience. This includes proper nutrition, regular exercise, and sufficient sleep.

Positive Relationships: Building strong, supportive relationships can provide emotional support and encouragement, enhancing resilience.

Coping Skills: Developing effective coping strategies, such as problem-solving and stress-management techniques, can enhance resilience.

Self-compassion: Self-compassion is treating oneself with care and understanding through times of hardship or perceived inadequacies, which assists in resilience.

Guides and Tips

Practice Mindfulness: Stay in the present moment. Instead of dwelling on past disappointments or fearing future uncertainties, focus on what can be done now.

Prioritize Self-care: Prioritize your physical health. Regular exercise, a well-balanced/ healthy diet, and adequate sleep may significantly influence your emotional health.

Foster Positive Relationships: Build relationships that provide support and encouragement. Surrounding yourself with positive influences can significantly boost your resilience.

Develop Effective Coping Skills: Learn strategies to handle stress and adversity more effectively. This can involve problem-solving techniques, stress management practices, or even seeking professional help if needed.

Practice Self-Compassion: Be nice and treat yourself with kindness and understanding. Instead of self-criticism, engage in self-compassion. Remember, everyone encounters setbacks.

To conclude, building emotional resilience is an ongoing process, which is critical in managing setbacks and growing from them. This involves developing the ability to adapt and recover from adversity, stress, and life's challenges. It's an ongoing, dynamic process that requires mindfulness, self-care, positive relationships, effective coping skills, and self-compassion and by fostering mindfulness, practising self-care, building supportive relationships, developing effective coping skills, and practising self-compassion, one can build a strong foundation of emotional resilience.

With emotional resilience, individuals are not only prepared to face career adversities but also equipped to thrive and succeed in their professional journeys.

Building emotional resilience is important in its contribution to stress management, healthy relationships, adaptability, career success, and overall well-being, making it a crucial factor in personal and professional success.

Key points to follow:

- The importance of mindfulness in emotional resilience
- The Role of physical health in emotional well-being
- The impact of positive Relationships on resilience
- The benefits of effective coping skills in managing adversity
- The role of self-compassion in resilience
- Identify what are your existing resilience factors and what areas need improvement.
- Explore what resources are available to improve emotional resilience and what obstacles could impede the building of resilience.

Chapter 4

FOSTERING A CAREER MANAGEMENT

Synopsis

Career management is a lifelong process of investing resources to achieve your career goals. It's not a one-time event but a series of actions to align your interests, skills, values, and personal circumstances with your work and organizational opportunities over your entire lifetime. Having a career management mindset involves:

- Taking an active and intentional approach to your career
- Continually assessing and developing your skills
- Setting goals
- Making informed decisions

This guide will explain the concepts behind fostering a career management mindset, provide multiple relevant examples, offer advice and tips, and include a check sheet format to help you cultivate this mindset effectively.

Fostering career management involves:

- *Planning your career path.*
- *Setting professional goals.*
- *Identifying learning and development opportunities.*
- *Making informed decisions about your career trajectory.*

It includes *proactive strategies to remain competitive in the labour market, such as continuing education, networking, improving professional skills, gaining new experiences, and staying aware of industry trends*.

Importance in Career-Shaping

Provides Direction: Career management helps you set clear career goals based on your interests, values, skills, and ambitions. It provides direction and focus, making your career progression more strategic and purposeful.

Enhances Employability: Active career management increases your employability. By staying on top of industry trends, expanding your skillset, and building a robust professional network, you enhance your marketability to potential employers.

Supports Career Satisfaction: Through career management, you align your career with your personal interests, values, and life circumstances. Increased job satisfaction, work-life balance, and general happiness can result from this alignment.

Encourages Lifelong Learning: Career management fosters a mindset of lifelong learning. You'll continually identify and pursue opportunities for skill development, knowledge enhancement, and professional growth.

Prepares for Change: Change is inevitable in today's dynamic job market. Career management prepares you to adapt to changes in the industry, economy, or personal circumstances. It enables you to navigate career transitions more effectively.

Drives Professional Growth: Career management propels your professional growth. You can achieve long-term career success by setting and achieving career goals, pursuing professional development opportunities, and seizing career-advancing opportunities.

Self-Assessment: Start by assessing your current skills, interests, values, and goals. Reflect on your strengths, weaknesses, and areas for improvement. Consider the following:

Skills: Identify your existing skills and determine which ones are transferable and relevant to your desired career path. For example: Skills-proficiency in project management, strong analytical abilities

Interests: Evaluate your passions and what truly motivates and excites you in a work setting.

Values: Define your core values and assess whether they align with your current or desired career.

Goals: Set clear short-term and long-term goals that align with your aspirations and values.

Interests: Passion for environmental sustainability, fascination with technology advancements

Values: Commitment to social responsibility, desire for work-life balance

Continuous Learning and Development: Embrace a lifelong learning mindset and actively seek opportunities for growth and development. This includes formal education, training programs, workshops, conferences, and self-directed learning.

Consider the following:

Stay Updated: Keep abreast of industry trends, technological advancements, and changes in your field.

Skill Enhancement: Identify skill gaps and take proactive steps to acquire new skills or improve existing ones.

Professional Networks: Build relationships with professionals in your industry to exchange knowledge and learn from others. Examples: Enroll in a coding boot camp to acquire programming skills.

Goal Setting and Planning: Set clear and actionable goals that align with your long-term career vision. Break down these goals into smaller, doable actions and steps to create a roadmap for success. Consider the following:

SMART Goals: Make sure your goals and objectives are specific, measurable, achievable, relevant, and time-bound.

Action Plans: Develop action plans for each goal, outlining the specific tasks, deadlines, and resources required.

Monitor Progress: Regularly review and track your progress towards your goals, making adjustments as needed.

Examples of SMART Goal setting:

Goal: Obtain a promotion to a managerial position within the next two years.

Action Plan: Enroll in leadership courses, take on additional responsibilities, and seek opportunities for mentorship and guidance.

Goal: Transition to a new industry within the next year

Action Plan: Conduct research on the new industry, acquire relevant skills through online courses or certifications, and network with professionals in the target industry.

Goals: Obtain a leadership position within five years and transition to a career that combines technology and sustainability.

Advice and Tips

1. Write down your goals and keep them visible as a constant reminder of your aspirations.
2. Regularly review and update your check sheet to align with your evolving career management mindset.
3. Break larger goals into smaller, manageable tasks to maintain motivation and momentum.
4. Celebrate milestones and achievements along the way to stay motivated and reinforce your progress.
5. Identify your strengths, internal factors that give you an advantage or set you apart from others. Assess your skills, experiences, personal qualities, and achievements, like strong leadership abilities, excellent problem-solving skills, effective communication and presentation skills.

6. Recognize your weaknesses, which are internal factors that hinder your progress or put you at a disadvantage. Identify areas where you may lack skills, experience, or confidence. (For example, limited expertise in project management, weaknesses in public speaking, Inadequate knowledge of a specific software tool, etc.)
7. Identify external opportunities that you can leverage to your advantage. These can include emerging trends, industry demands, networking connections, or professional development prospects. For example, there is a growing demand for professionals with data analytics skills, opportunities for advanced training in a specific programming language, networking events or conferences related to your field, etc.
8. Recognize external threats or challenges that may hinder your progress or pose risks to your career. These can include competition, economic factors, changing industry trends, or personal limitations. An example can be to cope with Increasing competition in your field of expertise, economic downturn affecting job opportunities, and rapidly evolving technology requiring continuous upskilling.
9. Be objective and honest when evaluating your strengths, weaknesses, opportunities, and threats.
10. Seek input from trusted mentors or colleagues to gain different perspectives.
11. Create a personalized learning plan that outlines your development goals and the steps needed to achieve them.

12. Seek for mentors or coaches who can guide and support your learning journey.
13. Evaluate your progress on a on a regular basis and alter your learning strategies as needed.
14. Attend industry conferences to keep up with the latest trends and developments.
15. Join professional associations or online communities related to your field for networking and learning opportunities.
16. Engage in self-reflection regularly to assess your skills, interests, values, and goals.
17. Seek feedback from mentors, colleagues, or career counsellors to gain additional insights.
18. Use assessment tools or online resources to support your self-assessment process.

Use the following check sheet format to track your self-assessment, learning and development, and goal setting.

Aspect	Description	Action Steps	Target Completion Date
Self-Assessment			
Learning and Development			
Goal Setting			

In conclusion, fostering career management is a proactive and strategic approach to shaping your career. It is about taking charge of your career path, making informed decisions, and pursuing growth opportunities. By managing your career effectively, you can not only achieve your professional goals but also attain career satisfaction and fulfilment. Career management, therefore, plays an essential role in shaping your career and is an ongoing process that continues throughout your professional life.

Chapter 5

REFLECTING ON YOUR PASSIONS: UNCOVER YOUR TRUE CAREER CALLING

Synopsis

In the realm of career development, aligning your passions and interests with your professional life is the cornerstone of fulfilment and success. It leads to increased motivation, better performance, and personal satisfaction. This chapter will guide you in exploring your passions and using them to unearth your true career calling. Reflecting on your passions to uncover your true career calling involves a deep and introspective journey to understand what truly drives you in life. It's discovering where your interests, values, skills, and motivations intersect and how they can be leveraged to carve out a fulfilling and sustainable career path.

Your passions can range from particular topics, hobbies, social causes, work tasks, and industries to environments where you feel most stimulated and satisfied. They are strong and consistent inclinations towards certain activities that provide you with a sense of enjoyment, fulfilment, and motivation.

Importance in Career-Shaping

Personal Fulfillment: When you follow your passions, you are more likely to feel fulfilled and satisfied with your work. Doing what you love can lead to a greater sense of purpose and happiness, ultimately enhancing your performance and career success.

Better Performance: Passion fosters enthusiasm and dedication, boosting your productivity, creativity, and willingness to go the extra mile. When you're passionate about your work, it no longer feels like a chore but an activity you genuinely enjoy and strive to excel in.

Resilience: Pursuing your passion helps you build resilience. You're more likely to overcome obstacles, endure setbacks, and navigate challenges when you're driven by passion and a strong sense of purpose.

Career Longevity: Careers based on passion will likely be more sustainable in the long run. You're more likely to stick with a career you love, even as you face inevitable challenges or industry shifts.

Professional Identity: Your professional identity can be shaped by your passions, helping you stand out in a competitive job market. When your career aligns with your passions, you're more likely to make a unique, authentic, and valuable contribution to your field.

1. Understanding Passion in the Career Context

Passion is a powerful force that may increase your career development and overall job satisfaction. The intense, enthusiastic interest or desire can motivate you, fuel your inspiration, and guide your career decisions. It often reveals itself as the activities, topics, or pursuits that you naturally gravitate towards and find intrinsically rewarding. Passion in a career context is about more than just loving what you do. It's about finding a career that connects with your values, interests, skills, and goals. When you align these aspects, you tap into a deep reservoir of motivation that can propel your career to new heights.

Understanding the Significance of Passion in Career Development

Passion is a powerful force that may propel your career development and overall job satisfaction. The intense, enthusiastic interest or desire can spark your motivation, fuel your inspiration, and guide your career decisions. It often reveals itself as the activities, topics, or pursuits that you naturally gravitate towards and find intrinsically rewarding.

Importance in Career-Shaping

Drives Motivation: Passion is a potent motivator. When you genuinely enjoy what you do, you are naturally inclined to give your best effort and strive for excellence. It pushes you to take the initiative, go the extra mile, and remain committed despite facing obstacles or setbacks.

Enhances Performance: Studies suggest a positive correlation between passion and job performance. When you are passionate about your work, you are more likely to be engaged, dedicated, and productive. This resonance enables you to approach your career with a sense of ownership and a personal stake, as you are no longer working to fulfil someone else's objectives but your own. You become more motivated, productive, and committed simply because your work is genuinely exciting and meaningful to you. Furthermore, you are more likely to continuously learn and improve, which can lead to higher competence and superior performance over time.

Boosts Job Satisfaction: Aligning your career with your passions can greatly enhance job satisfaction. When your career resonates with what you truly care about, it can lead to a higher sense of fulfilment, happiness, and well-being. When you're passionate about your work, you're likely to invest more effort and display a greater degree of persistence. This tenacity can be the difference between giving up when encountering hurdles and pushing through to find innovative solutions. The sense of achievement experienced in overcoming these challenges can feed back into your passion, creating a virtuous cycle of motivation and success.

This, in turn, can improve your overall job satisfaction and commitment to your career.

Promotes Career Resilience: Passion can bolster career resilience. It can give you the drive and determination to overcome career challenges, adapt to changes, and persist in the face of adversity. It helps you to keep going when things get tough and to bounce back from career setbacks or disappointments. Consider what you're naturally drawn to. What activities make you lose track of time? When do you feel most alive, engaged, and fulfilled? These reflections can provide valuable insights into your true passions.

Reflect on the times when you felt most motivated and successful in your career. Often, these are the times when you can align your work with your passions. Recognizing these instances can reaffirm the importance of passion in your career development and motivate you to continue seeking ways to incorporate your passions into your career.

Shapes Career Identity: Passion can shape your career identity. It can guide your career choices, define your professional role, and distinguish you in your field. When your career aligns with your passions, it reflects who you are, what you stand for, and where you want to go professionally. It's not just about doing what you love but also about finding fulfilment and meaning in what you do. Aligning your career with your passions allows you to tap into a profound source of energy and dedication, contributing to heightened work engagement, improved performance, and a deep sense of satisfaction.

Identifying Your Interests and Curiosities

The journey to a fulfilling career often begins with understanding your own interests and curiosities. This self-discovery process, far from being a simplistic exercise, is a profound introspection that can guide your career trajectory, improving job satisfaction, performance, and overall well-being.

Interests are what *you naturally gravitate towards, something you enjoy and find compelling. They are the activities, subjects, and tasks you are voluntarily drawn to beyond external incentives like money or recognition*. Interests can be broad-ranging, from a fascination with technology or finance to a love for arts or social services.

Curiosities, on the other hand, are *your natural inclinations to learn and explore. They can lead you towards new interests and open the door to creativity, innovation, and diverse perspectives*. Curiosity prompts the questioning of the status quo, incites the search for better solutions, and fosters continuous learning, which is vital in today's rapidly evolving career landscape.

Understanding the difference between interests and curiosities is important. Interests can form the foundation of your career—the baseline around which you can build your skills and expertise. Curiosities, however, drive evolution and growth. They push you to explore new avenues, acquire new skills, and thus provide the dynamic force that can prevent your career from stagnating.

First, they direct you towards career paths where you will naturally be more engaged and motivated, leading to higher job satisfaction and productivity. When you›re invested in your work, it no longer feels like a chore but becomes a source of joy and fulfilment.

Second, in a world where differentiation is key, aligning your career with your unique blend of interests and curiosities can make you stand out. It allows you to build an authentic and unique personal brand, offering genuine value to your employers or clients.

Third, understanding your interests and curiosities can make your career resilient in the face of change. In an era of technological breakthroughs and unpredictable job market trends, curiosities can guide you towards acquiring future-relevant skills and keep your career progressing.

Reflecting on Your Passions: A Step-by-Step Guide

Step 1: Self-Assessment: Identify what you love doing. This could be activities that make you lose track of time, themes in the books and articles you read, or topics you love discussing.

Step 2: Identify Skills and Talents: Reflect on your abilities and strengths. What are you naturally good at? What skills have you developed over time?

Step 3: Evaluate Your Values: What's important to you? What impact do you want to make in the world?

Step 4: Explore Career Paths: Look at various careers that align with your passions, skills, and values.

Step 5: Experiment and Learn: Gain exposure to your areas of interest through internships, volunteer work, courses, or side projects.

Uncovering Your Career Calling: An Example

Let's take Anna, who loves storytelling, has a knack for writing, values creativity, and wants to inspire people. Reflecting on these aspects, she could uncover her true calling to become a writer or a content creator. Anna could take a creative writing course, start a blog, or intern at a publishing house to gain more clarity.

Here are some tips to guide you on this journey:

Patience is Key: Finding your true career calling can take time. Be patient with the process.

Passion Exploration: Identify your passions and interests.

Experiment and gain experience.

Maintain a Growth Mindset: Adopting a growth mindset means recognizing that your abilities and intelligence can be developed through effort, learning, and persistence. It's about viewing challenges as opportunities to grow rather than as insurmountable obstacles. This attitude can help you adapt to change and stay open to learning throughout your life.

Stay Curious: Curiosity is the bedrock of lifelong learning. Ask questions, seek answers, and explore new topics, tools, or methods in your field. Curiosity can also lead to innovation and creativity, which are highly valuable in today's evolving job market.

Commit to Continuous Learning: Make learning a regular part of your routine. This can involve attending seminars and webinars, taking up online courses, reading industry-specific books, or even staying up-to-date with your field's news and trends.

Embrace Change: Change is often uncomfortable, but it's also inevitable. By developing resilience and learning to see change as an opportunity rather than a threat, you can adapt more effectively when new situations or challenges arise.

Develop Versatility: Develop a diverse set of transferable skills, such as problem-solving, communication, leadership and critical thinking. This not only makes you more adaptable to change but also opens up new career opportunities.

Find Mentors and Role Models: Look for people who are where you want to be in your career. Their journeys can provide valuable insights, inspiration, and practical tips on navigating change and continuing learning.

Network: Building strong professional relationships can provide opportunities to learn from others, gain different perspectives, and discover new opportunities. It's also a good way to stay informed about changes in your industry.

Reflect Regularly: Take time to reflect on your career path, skills, interests, and goals. This can help you identify areas where you need to adapt or learn more and guide your personal and professional growth.

Accept Failure as Part of the Learning Process: Don't be afraid to fail. Every failure offers a learning opportunity. It's an essential part of growth and leads to resilience. Remember, your career is not just about making a living—it's about making a life. So, dive deep into your passions, reflect on your strengths and values, and uncover a career that excites you to get up in the morning. When your passion and career align, the result is a life that's not only successful but also profoundly satisfying.

In this chapter, you have embarked on a journey of self-reflection to uncover your true career calling. By exploring your passions, aligning with your values, and leveraging your strengths, you have gained clarity and direction in shaping a fulfilling career. Remember to seek guidance, embrace the journey, and remain open to new possibilities as you uncover your true career calling. With authenticity and passion as your guide, you are on the path to unleashing your full potential and finding profound fulfilment in your professional life.

Chapter 6

EMBRACING GROWTH MINDSET: CULTIVATING A LEARNING ATTITUDE

Synopsis

Embracing Growth Mindset: Cultivating a learning attitude is a holistic concept that involves adopting a positive mindset and a continuous learning approach to life and career. It's a shift from a fixed mindset, which sees abilities as innate and unchangeable, to a growth mindset, which believes that abilities can be developed through dedication and hard work. This refers to adopting a psychological framework that perceives challenges as opportunities for learning and growth rather than obstacles. Developed by psychologist Carol Dweck, the 'growth mindset' concept contrasts with a 'fixed mindset,' which assumes that our abilities, intelligence, and talents are static traits.

A growth mindset believes that your basic traits, such as intelligence or talent, are merely starting points for your development and that you can cultivate these through your efforts. This perspective creates a love for learning and a resilience that is vital for significant accomplishment in all areas of life, including career. They recognize that they may not be able to do something "yet," but they understand that they can learn and improve with time, effort, and persistence. Failure is viewed as a motivator for growth and expanding current talents rather than as evidence of incompetence.

In contrast, **a fixed mindset f**osters a fear of failure, avoidance of challenges, and the belief that talent alone leads to success. These individuals might believe that if you need to work hard at something, then you must not be good at it.

Embracing a growth mindset involves understanding that there›s always room for improvement and that every experience provides an opportunity to learn. It›s about being flexible and adaptive, seeking feedback, and seeing failure not as evidence of a lack of intelligence or ability but as a catalyst for growth and stretching existing skills. It leads to an attitude where challenges are welcomed, and effort is seen as the pathway to mastery.

Cultivating a learning attitude is an integral part of embracing a growth mindset. It means committing to continuous self-improvement, being open-minded, and being willing to learn from all experiences—good or bad. It involves staying curious, asking questions, and seeking knowledge. It also means being receptive to feedback and viewing it as a tool for growth, not as criticism.

The significance of embracing a growth mindset and cultivating a learning attitude in shaping one's career cannot be overemphasized. It leads to higher motivation levels, improved productivity, greater resilience, and adaptability to change—all key factors for success in today's rapidly evolving job market. A professional with a growth mindset is better equipped to handle career challenges, adapt to new situations, learn new skills, and achieve their career goals. They are more likely to perceive challenges as opportunities rather than obstacles. They are better at problem-solving, making them valuable assets in any work environment.

On the other hand, a learning attitude ensures career longevity. As industries and job roles continually evolve, to stay relevant, professionals need to keep updating their skills and knowledge. Those who are committed to learning are more likely to remain employable and less likely to become obsolete in their careers.

The significance of embracing a growth mindset and cultivating a learning attitude is manifold.

Enhanced Learning: A growth mindset encourages a love for learning and perseverance that is crucial for significant accomplishments.

Better Performance: Studies have shown that students and employees with a growth mindset persist in facing challenges, leading to better performance over time.

Increased Creativity: A growth mindset encourages risk-taking and innovation, leading to higher levels of creativity.

Resilience: A growth mindset fosters resilience, allowing individuals to bounce back from failures and adversities more effectively.

Career Progression: A learning attitude opens opportunities for personal development, skill acquisition, and career progression.

Embracing a growth mindset involves changing one's belief about learning and growth. It means understanding that intelligence and abilities can be developed, learning to appreciate the process of learning, valuing effort, responding to failures and challenges with resilience, and seeking and utilizing feedback for improvement.

Fostering a growth mindset involves believing that skills, abilities, and intelligence are not fixed traits but can be developed over time. This belief can significantly shape a person's personal and professional life, making them more resilient, motivated, and successful. Let's dive into the specifics, using Robert, an aspiring entrepreneur, as an example.

Key points to consider:

- **Believe in Change**: The foundation and concept at the heart of a growth mindset is the belief that abilities can change. Understand that the brain is malleable, and with consistent effort, you can improve.
- **Value Effort Over** Talent: A growth mindset involves recognizing that effort is a path to mastery, not a sign of weakness. Remember, natural talent without hard work seldom leads to success.

- **Embrace Challenges**: Welcome challenges as opportunities to learn and grow rather than viewing them as threats.
- **Learn from Criticism**: Use criticism as a tool for self-improvement rather than viewing it as an attack.
- **Celebrate Growth**: Find joy in the journey and celebrate small wins along the way.
- **The transformative power** of believing in change. What hinders you from adopting a growth mindset?
- **The value of effort and perseverance**. What resources can help you cultivate a growth mindset?
- **The benefits of embracing challenges**. What are your existing strengths that support a growth mindset?
- **The importance of learning from criticism**. What obstacles could impede the development of a growth mindset?

To conclude, embracing a growth mindset and cultivating a learning attitude is pivotal to career success. Changing how we perceive abilities and intelligence, valuing effort, embracing challenges, learning from criticism, and celebrating growth can enhance resilience, motivation, and success in our careers. This, coupled with the understanding that failure isn't a dead-end but an opportunity for learning and growth, will help individuals like Robert thrive in their professional journeys.

Chapter 7

IDENTIFYING YOUR CORE VALUES: BUILDING A SOLID FOUNDATION FOR CAREER SATISFACTION

Synopsis

Identifying your core values and building a solid foundation for career satisfaction is a conceptual framework that posits the alignment of personal core values with professional life as a vital element for achieving career satisfaction and success. Your core values are the deeply ingrained principles that guide your decisions, actions, and attitudes. They reflect what is genuinely essential to you, serving as a compass that directs your behaviour and action, shaping your goals and giving your life and work meaning.

Examples of core values can range widely and may include honesty, integrity, creativity, innovation, service, diversity, education, respect, family, and many more. They represent what we stand for, influencing our goals, priorities, and the directions we choose to pursue.

Identifying your core values means discerning what is genuinely essential to you, introspection and self-analysis to determine what truly matters to you, what you believe in, and what shapes your character. It's a process of uncovering what drives your decisions, motivates you, and makes you happy. This process often involves asking probing questions, reflecting on times when you felt most satisfied and fulfilled, and identifying the common threads in those experiences. These could include values like honesty, creativity, family, service to others, personal growth, health, independence, or financial security, among others. In essence, they are your guiding principles in life.

Why is this important in shaping your career? The simple answer is alignment. When your career aligns with your core values, you are more likely to find satisfaction and fulfilment in your work. You're more likely to invest yourself fully in your tasks, resulting in higher productivity, improved performance, and increased job satisfaction. For instance, if one of your core values is service to others, you might find a career in social work, healthcare, or customer service deeply satisfying.

Building a solid foundation for career satisfaction refers to establishing a career that is not only professionally rewarding but also personally fulfilling. When you align your career path with your core values, you are more likely to experience satisfaction, as your professional life will reflect what is truly important to you, leading to a sense of purpose and meaning.

The importance of identifying your core values and aligning them with your career path can be seen in several ways.

Increased Job Satisfaction: When your career aligns with your core values, you find greater meaning and fulfilment in your work, leading to increased job satisfaction.

Better Decision-Making: Knowing your core values can guide your decisions, ensuring they are consistent with what matters most to you.

Improved Performance and Success: When you are passionate about your work and find it meaningful, you will likely be more dedicated, motivated, and perform better.

Greater Work-Life Balance: Aligning your career with your core values can lead to a better work-life balance as your career does not feel 'out of sync' with your personal life.

Following a career path that aligns with your values can contribute to your personal growth and development, as your work will enable you to express and further develop your values.

Therefore, identifying your core values and building a solid foundation for career satisfaction involves understanding your fundamental beliefs and aligning them with your career path. This alignment is crucial in driving job satisfaction, improving decision-making, enhancing performance and success, achieving a work-life balance, and promoting personal growth and development. In essence, by identifying and adhering to your core values, you lay a solid foundation for a rewarding and satisfying career. Identifying your core values is a vital step in building a solid foundation for career satisfaction. The fundamental beliefs that influence and guide our behaviours and decision-making processes are core values.

Here's how you can identify and leverage your core values:

1. Reflection:

The first step in identifying your core values is reflection. Think about the situations when you were most proud, fulfilled, or satisfied.

Example: You may recall standing up for a colleague or completing a challenging project. The values that come up in these memories, like fairness, resilience, or diligence, might be your core values.

Advice: This reflection should not be rushed. Take time to explore your memories and emotions.

2. List Your Values:

After reflecting on your experiences, jot down the values that resonate with you.

Example: You might write down values like honesty, creativity, independence, ambition, and loyalty.

Advice: This List doesn›t need to be perfect or definitive. It›s just a starting point.

3. Prioritize Your Values:

Once you have your List, prioritize these values based on their importance to you.

Example: If you value both honesty and ambition but would choose to be honest even if it meant missing a lucrative opportunity, then honesty ranks higher than ambition for you.

Advice: Prioritizing your values helps you understand which ones are genuinely core to who you are.

4. Align Your Values with Your Career:

Finally, find ways to integrate your values into your career.

Example: If one of your core values is creativity, you might seek out projects or roles that allow for innovative thinking and problem-solving.

Advice: When you're more likely to work aligns with your values, you will likely find satisfaction and fulfilment.

Opportunities: Are there ways you could better align your career with your values? If you value helping others, perhaps there›s an opportunity to transition into a mentoring role.

Threats: Are there aspects of your job that conflict with your values? If one of your values is work-life balance, but your job requires long hours, this might threaten your career satisfaction.

Checklist for identifying core values:

- Reflect on past experiences and emotions.
- List potential core values.

- Prioritize your values.
- Align your values with your career.
- Conduct a SWOT analysis to evaluate the interplay between your core values and professional life.

On the contrary, if your career does not align with your core values, it could lead to job dissatisfaction, stress, and burnout. For example, if your core value is work-life balance, but you're in a job that demands 80-hour work weeks, it's likely to result in stress and unhappiness.

Identifying and honouring your core values can provide a solid foundation for career satisfaction. It allows you to make choices that resonate with who you are at a fundamental level, leading to more significant alignment and fulfilment in your professional life.

Chapter 8

SETTING MEANINGFUL GOALS: CREATING A ROADMAP TO CAREER SUCCESS

Synopsis

Setting meaningful goals involves identifying what you want to achieve in your career, why these achievements are significant to you, and how you plan to accomplish them. These goals should be SMART: Specific, Measurable, Achievable, Relevant, and Time-bound. They provide direction and a sense of purpose, ensuring your career development efforts are focused and strategic.

This concept emphasizes the importance of setting intentional, well-defined, and purposeful goals to achieve career success. The premise of this idea is that career success doesn't occur by chance but results from strategic planning and action.

Creating a roadmap to career success is about laying out a step-by-step plan to reach your career goals. It involves defining the necessary steps, identifying potential obstacles, developing strategies to overcome these obstacles, and setting a timeline for achieving these goals. It provides clarity and guides your decision-making processes.

The importance of setting meaningful goals and creating a roadmap to career success can be seen in several ways:

Direction and Focus: Clear goals provide guidance, helping you focus your time, energy, and resources on what's important, which increases productivity and effectiveness.

Motivation and Commitment: Having meaningful goals that resonate with your values and aspirations can boost your motivation and commitment, driving you to persist in facing challenges.

Measurement of Progress: Goals give you a benchmark to measure your progress. By regularly reviewing your goals, you can adjust your strategies as needed, ensuring you stay on the right track.

Enhanced Decision-Making: When you have clear goals, making decisions aligned with your career objectives is simpler.

Career Satisfaction and Success: Achieving goals you've set for yourself brings a sense of accomplishment and satisfaction, contributing to overall career success.

Goal setting is a critical component of career success. You can design a roadmap that guides your professional growth by establishing clear, achievable objectives.

Here's how to set meaningful career goals:

1. Define Your Career Aspirations:

This is identifying your long-term career goals and what you want to achieve professionally. It involves introspection and self-reflection to understand your interests, strengths, and passions. Defining your career aspirations provides a clear vision for your future, guiding your decisions and actions towards your desired career path. Start by considering your career aspirations. What role or position do you want to achieve in the long term?

Example: You may be a software engineer now, but your long-term goal could be to become a chief technology officer.

Advice: Consider your interests, values, and passions when defining your career aspirations. Be ambitious but also realistic.

2. Set S.M.A.R.T Goals:

Once you've defined your career aspirations, setting Specific, Measurable, Achievable, Relevant, and Time-bound (S.M.A.R.T) goals is critical. These clear, well-defined targets act as stepping stones towards your career aspirations.

Specific, Measurable, Achievable, Relevant, and Time-bound (S.M.A.R.T) goals can provide clear steps towards achieving your long-term career aspirations. An S.M.A.R.T goal could be to "obtain a project management certification within the following year."

Example: "Increase my coding speed by 20% in the next six months by attending a coding boot camp and practising for an hour daily."

Advice: Write down your S.M.A.R.T. goals and review them regularly. This keeps them at the forefront of your mind and allows you to track your progress.

3. Break Down Goals:

Significant, long-term goals can be overwhelming. Breaking them down into smaller, doable tasks makes them more attainable and less intimidating. This involves creating a roadmap or action plan detailing the specific steps, resources, and timelines needed to achieve your goals. Divide your long-term goals down into smaller, short-term goals. This makes them more manageable and less overwhelming.

Example: If your goal is to become a project manager, a short-term goal could be to lead a small project or team.

Advice: Consider what steps you need to take to achieve your long-term goal and turn these into your short-term goals.

4. Seek Feedback:

Feedback is an essential component of career development. It provides a reality check, helping you understand your progress towards your goals, your strengths, and areas for improvement. You can seek feedback from various sources, including mentors, supervisors, peers, or through self-assessment. Constructive feedback can guide your learning and improvement, ensuring you're on the right track towards your career aspirations. Regular feedback can provide valuable insights into your performance and progress towards your goals.

Example: If one of your goals is to improve your presentation skills, seek feedback from colleagues or superiors after each presentation you give.

> **Key things to consider:**
> - Be open to both positive and constructive Feedback, and use it to adjust your goals and strategies if needed.
> - What do you excel at that will help you achieve your goals?
> - What areas do you need to improve on to reach your goals?
> - What opportunities can you exploit to help you meet your goals?
> - Define your career aspirations.
> - Set S.M.A.R.T goals.
> - Break down long-term goals into short-term goals.
> - Seek regular Feedback on your progress.
> - Conduct a SWOT analysis related to your goals.
> - Regularly review and alter your goals based on your progress and any changes in your circumstances or aspirations.

Remember, goal setting is a dynamic process. Revising your goals as your interests, skills, and circumstances change is okay. Stay flexible, and remember to celebrate your achievements along the way. This involves establishing well-defined, purposeful, achievable goals guiding your career path. The creation of a detailed plan helps ensure that these goals are realized. The importance of this process lies in its ability to provide direction and focus, motivate and commit, measure progress, enhance decision-making, and ultimately lead to career satisfaction and success. In essence, setting meaningful goals and creating a roadmap is a strategic approach to navigating one's career journey effectively.

Chapter 9

SEEKING MENTORSHIP: TAPPING INTO THE POWER OF GUIDANCE AND SUPPORT

Synopsis

Seeking Mentorship: Tapping into the power of guidance and support" is an imperative principle that underscores the significance of obtaining guidance, knowledge, and encouragement from more experienced individuals (mentors) to foster personal and professional growth. The process of seeking mentorship involves identifying individuals who have the expertise, wisdom, and practical experience from which one can learn and grow.

Mentorship involves a relationship between a mentor (an experienced and trusted individual) and a mentee (the person being mentored). The mentor gives advice, shares knowledge and expertise, and supports the mentee's personal and professional development. The essence of mentorship is about leveraging the mentor's experience to guide one's journey, providing insight and perspective that might not be gained otherwise. Mentorship is a powerful tool for career growth. Mentors can provide guidance, share their experiences, and offer valuable feedback, helping you navigate your career journey more effectively.

Tapping into the power of guidance and support means recognizing mentorship's value and actively seeking it out. It's about harnessing the wisdom, knowledge, skills, and experiences of others to help navigate one's path, particularly in areas such as career progression, skill development, problem-solving, and overcoming challenges.

The importance of seeking mentorship and tapping into the power of guidance and support can be recognized in several ways.

Here's how to seek and maximize mentorship:

Accelerated Learning: Mentors can provide invaluable knowledge and insights, helping mentees avoid common pitfalls and hasten their learning process.

Expanded Network: Mentors can help boost your professional network, introducing you to other professionals in your field, potential employers, or business opportunities. This can open doors to career advancements and collaborations that might otherwise remain closed.

Improved Skills/Skill Development: By observing your mentor and through their guidance, you can learn and develop vital skills. This could range from technical skills specific to your industry to soft skills such as leadership, communication, problem-solving, and more. Through their advice and feedback, mentors can help mentees improve essential skills, such as leadership, communication, decision-making, and problem-solving.

Enhanced Self-awareness: Mentors can provide constructive feedback, aiding in self-reflection and self-improvement.

Increased Confidence: By validating the mentee's ideas and efforts, a mentor can help build the mentee's confidence and self-esteem.

Career Advancement: Mentorship can provide insights and opportunities that significantly influence career progression, helping the mentee to climb the career ladder faster. A mentor can assist you in defining your career goals, planning your career path, and making informed career decisions. They can give constructive feedback and help you identify areas for improvement, thereby aiding your career progression.

Guidance and Advice: Mentors often have a wealth of industry experience and can offer practical advice on navigating professional challenges. They can provide insights into industry trends, career opportunities, and strategies for professional growth that you may not be aware of or may overlook.

Support and Encouragement: Mentors can be a source of moral support, helping to boost your confidence and motivation. They can provide encouragement during tough times, share their own experiences of overcoming challenges, and inspire you to persevere in your career journey.

Identify Potential Mentors: The first step towards seeking mentorship involves identifying the right mentor. This individual should ideally be someone who aligns with your career aspirations, possesses the skills and knowledge you wish to acquire, and embodies the values and professional ethos you admire. They could be a senior colleague, industry leader, or even a professional from a different but relevant field. A potential mentor could also challenge your thinking and encourage growth. The process of identifying potential mentors involves:

- Self-reflection on your career goals.
- Research on potential mentors.
- A careful evaluation of how their guidance could shape your career path.

A good mentor is someone who has experience or skills that align with your career goals. They should be someone you respect and whose guidance you value.

Example: If you aspire to be a successful entrepreneur, a seasoned business owner in your industry could make an excellent mentor.

Advice: When identifying potential mentors, consider their experience, skills, values, and willingness to mentor.

Approach Potential Mentors: Once potential mentors are identified, the next step involves approaching them tactfully.

This is a crucial step and should be carried out professionally and respectfully. It's essential to express your admiration for their work, clearly communicate your objectives for seeking mentorship, and highlight what you believe both parties can gain from this relationship. Remember, the aim is to build a relationship based on mutual respect and shared interest, so honesty and sincerity are essential.

When approaching a potential mentor, be respectful and clear about why you seek their mentorship.

Example: You might say, «I admire your success in the tech industry, and I believe I could learn a lot from your experiences. Would you be open to discussing a potential mentorship?»

Advice: Respect their time and show that you're serious about learning and growing.

Make the Most of Mentorship: It's crucial to utilize this opportunity fully after establishing the mentor-mentee relationship. This involves:

- Actively seeking advice
- Being open to feedback
- Implementing the mentor's suggestions
- Continually learning from their experience

Regular interactions, respecting the mentor's time, being prepared with questions, and demonstrating progress can help derive maximum benefit from the mentorship.

Once you have a mentor, be proactive in seeking their advice, setting goals for what you want to achieve, and working on their feedback.

Example: If your mentor advises you to improve your public speaking skills, you might join a local Toastmasters club to practice and improve.

Advice: Always prepare for your meetings with your mentor. Have specific points you want to discuss or questions you want to ask.

Show Gratitude: Lastly, expressing gratitude towards your mentor is vital. Mentors devote their time and energy to supporting your growth, so acknowledging their effort and showing appreciation is essential. This can be done through simple thank you messages, sharing updates about your progress and achievements, or occasional gifts. Express your appreciation for your mentor's time and advice regularly.

Example: You could say, «I just wanted to thank you for your advice on handling client meetings. It really made a difference at my presentation yesterday.»

Advice: A slight note of thanks, a sincere verbal thank you, or even a token gift can go a long way in showing your appreciation.

In summary, seeking mentorship and tapping into the power of guidance and support is about recognizing the value of learning from those who have traversed the path before you and actively pursuing relationships with these individuals. The importance of this concept lies in the accelerated learning, expanded network, improved skills, enhanced self-awareness, increased confidence, and career advancement that mentorship can provide. As such, seeking mentorship is crucial to personal and career development strategies.

Remember, mentorship is a two-way street. While mentors provide valuable guidance, mentees must also try to learn, grow, and make the most of the mentorship relationship.

Printed in the USA
CPSIA information can be obtained
at www.ICGtesting.com
LVHW041318140524
780251LV00002B/296

9 789356 488710